Gender in Securitization Theory

INTERKULTURELLER DIALOG

Edited by Annemarie Profanter

VOLUME 13

Camilla Vianini

Gender in Securitization Theory

A feminist analysis of smuggling and trafficking governance in the EU

PETER LANG

Berlin · Bruxelles · Chennai · Lausanne · New York · Oxford

Bibliographic Information published by the Deutsche Nationalbibliothek
The Deutsche Nationalbibliothek lists this publication in the Deutsche Nationalbibliografie;
detailed bibliographic data is available online at http://dnb.d-nb.de.

Library of Congress Control Number: 2025031610

Cover photo: Woman in Hijab Talking with Girl, photo by Ahmed akacha, retrieved from
Pexels (https://www.pexels.com/photo/woman-in-hijab-talking-with-girl-10629468/).

ISSN 1866-752X
ISBN 978-3-631-94273-4 (Print)
ISBN 978-3-631-94274-1 (ePDF)
ISBN 978-3-631-94275-8 (ePUB)
DOI 10.3726/b23197

© 2026 Peter Lang Group AG, Lausanne (Switzerland)
Published by Peter Lang GmbH, Berlin (Germany)

info@peterlang.com

www.peterlang.com

Table of Contents

Context

"Securitization theory is sexist" (Gomes & Marques, 2021, p. 79). This was the crude criticism directed by feminist scholars towards the long-standing theory that has defined critical security studies since the end of the Cold War. The "striking absence" (Hansen, 2000, p. 286) of gender was first denounced by Lene Hansen in 2000. Since then, the Copenhagen School has collected increasing critiques regarding its gender blindness and inability to consider gender as a significant factor in the securitization process. Scholars argue that this neglect contributes to the perpetuation of sexism within securitized policies and negatively impacts the experiences of women and men in real life. Thus, it is imperative to address it. Gomes and Marques (2021) suggest that "to overcome the sexist neglect of securitization theory, there is a need for empirical studies recognizing gender (and race) as structural conditions" (p. 79).

Therefore, it is crucial to recognize gender as an essential factor in the securitization process. In particular, this monograph focuses on the most popular application of securitization theory: migration. While the gendered implications of securitized migration policies have been the subject of several recent analyses (Freedman, 2016, 2019; Luthman, 2017), few studies have explored the role of gender in the securitization of policies on migration management, creating a significant knowledge gap. This monograph aims to fill such a gap by answering the research question: *How does gender influence the securitization of migration in the European Union (EU)?* The research seeks to overcome the gender-blind approach prevalent in the Copenhagen School's securitization theory from a post-colonial feminist tradition.

In particular, the aim is to identify "which gendered (and racialized) crisis narratives are institutionally anchored and inscribed" (Sachseder et al., 2022, p. 6) into the migration management architecture of the EU. On the basis of previous literature, gendered and racialized constructions of threat and vulnerability are believed to mutually reinforce the securitization of migration policies in the EU. The research aims to find how, on the one hand, the perceived vulnerability of refugee women has been framed as a referent object in the EU's securitization process by drawing from theories of humanitarian securitization and, on the other hand, how migrant men have been securitized in light of their alleged dangerousness. The construction of refugees as both threats and in need of protection can be explained through gender lenses, with the implementation of masculinized notions of dangerousness and feminized perceptions of vulnerability. The successful securitization of migration in the EU is argued to rely on gendered constructions of femininity and masculinity.

While previous research has examined how these gendered constructions are perpetuated in some areas of EU migration governance – namely, through the analysis of the policies of Frontex (Stachowitsch & Sachseder, 2019) and the European Agenda on Migration (Welfens, 2020) –, a central piece of EU border management has never been addressed in the context of the gendered influence on migration's securitization. Smuggling and trafficking governance are crucial instruments of border control and migration management and are thus selected as the case study of the monograph. The EU has developed increasingly supranational competencies on smuggling and trafficking as part of the Europeanization of migration and the communitarization of border control, engaging in a 'war against smugglers and traffickers' that has received renewed attention since the 2015 refugee crisis. These phenomena have been securitized and framed as threats to the EU's internal security and to the migrant victims of the crimes. A Critical Frame Analysis is conducted in order to understand whether and how gendered constructions of vulnerability and masculinity have affected smuggling and trafficking policies.

The context sections provides a comprehensive literature review of the critical concepts of securitization, gender, and securitized migration. Combining gender studies with securitization theory, the paragraph retraces previous literature's findings on how gendered (and racialized) constructions of threat

CONTEXT

and vulnerability mutually reinforce the securitization process within EU migration policies.

1.1 Securitization theory

According to Buzan et al. (1998), any issue is located on a spectrum that ranges from non-politicized through politicized to securitized, and can be moved from one end to the other according to the specific process of 'securitization'. The positioning of an issue on the spectrum is determined by the level of threat it poses to a referent object and the type of reaction it elicits by the state as provider of security. An issue that is 'non-politicized' is not present in the public debate as such and the state is not involved in managing it. A 'politicized' issue is considered a matter of public policy and is regulated by the state's non-military instruments. Finally, an issue that has been securitized is presented as an existential threat that calls for the state to intervene with extraordinary measures, including military ones. The process which moves an issue towards the right-end of the spectrum is securitization. Successful securitization is comprised of three steps: (1) framing existential threats, (2) mobilizing emergency action, (3) breaking free of rules of interunit relations (Buzan et al., 1998).

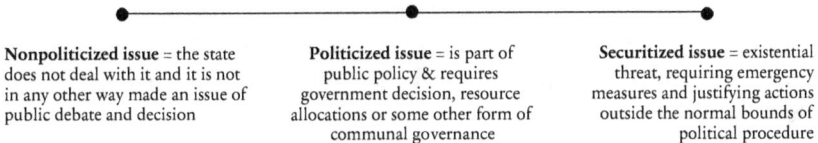

Nonpoliticized issue = the state does not deal with it and it is not in any other way made an issue of public debate and decision	Politicized issue = is part of public policy & requires government decision, resource allocations or some other form of communal governance	Securitized issue = existential threat, requiring emergency measures and justifying actions outside the normal bounds of political procedure

Political and public discourses frame an issue as 'above politics' in order to elicit a response from the state which mobilizes means beyond the ordinary political ones. The concept of securitization can be considered an extreme version of politicization (Hudson, 2005). The justification to mobilize exceptional resources lies in the argument that the to-be-securitized issue has absolute priority over others because it poses an existential threat to a referent object. It is important to note that in the Copenhagen School's understanding, security is a self-referential practice. This means that it is impossible to objectively identify what poses an existential threat to a particular referent object; what matters is the definition of the issue as a threat that requires emergency action.

The framing of the existential threat happens through discourse. Buzan et al. (1998) draw from language theory and employ the figure of 'speech act' to describe the process by which elites speak the existential threat into existence. They explain that "it is the utterance itself that is the act; by saying the words, something is done" (Buzan et al., 1998, p. 26). First, the speech act highlights how an issue poses an existential threat to the status quo, the state, society, or a different referent object. Secondly, it emphasizes that a point of no return has been reached where all ordinary measures are unable to solve the issue. Finally, it presents a possible way out that requires the employment of extraordinary measures, including the legitimate use of force.

A speech act can be more or less successful depending on some facilitating conditions, such as the characteristics of the issue itself or the social capital of the elite performing the speech act. It is usually the political elites and the media that assume the role of 'securitizing actor'. A speech act is successful when the framing of the issue as an existential threat and the call to action for the employment of out-of-ordinary resources is accepted by the audience. The speech act and its acceptance by the audience together comprise the 'securitizing move'. The audience is usually comprised of the general public. Its role is often underestimated compared to that of the securitizing actors, with the latter privileged and the former marginalized. However, without acceptance from the audience a securitizing move is doomed to fail.

1.2 Gender as an analytical category

The second main concept on which the research is based, together with securitization theory and migration, is that of gender. Gender is at the core of feminist studies. What is gender? The term gained popularity in the social sciences in the mid-1970s when it was already widely used to indicate the social construction of femininities and masculinities. Differentiated from biological sex, it indicates the different socially learned and cultural behaviors about what it means to be a man (masculinity) and what it means to be a woman (femininity) (Hudson, 2005). At the end of the 1980s, scholars recognized that gender was "fluid and not polar, relational and performative" (Donato et al., 2006, p. 5). While sex is assigned at birth, gender is a subjective process that can change over time.

It is important to consider an intersectional understanding of gender in the study. The concept of intersectionality was originally coined by feminist scholar Kimberlé Crenshaw (1991) who identified how the interaction between the patriarchal, racist, and capitalist social structures dominating modern society produces a particularly severe type of marginalization. The marginalization is defined as "contingent and relational" (Welfens, 2020, p. 514), because it is always relative to the context. As brilliantly illustrated by Turner (2016), "a person is not vulnerable because they are a man or a woman, but because of what being a man or a woman means in particular situations". Post-colonial feminist scholar Chandra Talapade Mohanty (1984) maintains that an intersectional understanding of gender needs to be integrated into all feminist studies. Her approach is particularly relevant to this work since it concerns women and migration, thus referring to racialized women migrants from the Global South.

According to post-colonial feminism, the intersection of gender and race produces an additional level of marginalization for racialized women. Even within feminist theory, women from the Global South or, in general, women of color have often been represented as a monolithic group, characterized by extreme vulnerability and even backwardness. Western feminists eagerly bought into the construction of 'third-world women' as 'powerless,' 'exploited', and 'sexually harassed' (Schrover, 2019). Mohanty (1984) explains that the narrative of 'sexually constrained' and from the 'Third World' is interpreted as meaning that non-Western women are "ignorant, poor, uneducated, tradition-bound, domestic, family-oriented, victimized" (p. 65).

These gendered and racist assumptions have been integrated into the modern colonial project as justifications for modern expansions or interventions, with a infamous example being the 2003 invasion of Iraq by the United States (Kebsi, 2021). Elites in the Global North have relied on orientalist stereotypes to narrate non-Western, non-white populations as 'backwards' and 'threatening'. Within these contexts, local women are perceived as victims of the violent and oppressive cultural norms supposedly perpetuated by local men (Gray & Franck, 2019). The West poses itself as a liberator with "white men saving brown women from brown men" (Spivak, 1988).

1.3 The great absent in securitization studies: gender

"Securitization theory is sexist" (Gomes & Marques, 2021, p. 79). This was the crude criticism directed by feminist scholars towards the long-standing theory that has defined critical security studies since the end of the Cold War. The "striking absence of gender" (Hansen, 2000, p. 286) in securitization theory was only challenged for the first time by Hansen (2000). She put forward a feminist critique of securitization theory, which was aimed at deepening the Copenhagen School's understanding of security. Including gender as well as race in the theory leads to a more complex and layered understanding of the power relations that produce securitization and of the consequences of such a process for all involved or ignored actors (Gomes & Marques, 2021). Hansen (2000) criticizes the methodological limits of securitization theory and identifies two blind spots in the process.

According to Gomes and Marques (2021), sexism and racism in securitization theory can be overcome if gender and race are finally recognized as structural features in the securitization process. They find that so far studies have maintained a supposed 'neutrality' of the process, that is nothing other than the perpetuation of patriarchal and colonial hierarchies as the normal state of affairs, in line with the dominant "malestreaming" (Hudson, 2005, p. 160) of security studies. A possible solution proposed by Gomes and Marques (2021) is to apply Maria Lugones (2010)'s framework of the colonial/modern gender system to securitization theory. The framework maintains that patriarchy, racism, and capitalism are the main social structures constructed over time on the basis of historical colonialism that constitute society today. The three social structures intersectionally interact with each other to produce the social categories of gender, race, and class. In turn, these categories "segregate and hierarchize" (Gomes & Marques, 2021, p. 81) social groups, with some being marginalized and others elevated to a position of dominance.

The intersection between the different axes of inequality co-creates a particular instance of marginalization (Crenshaw, 1991). Such hierarchies are reflected in the securitization process, with the elites at the top having the power to define what or who is a threat and what or who must be protected. The discursive nature of securitization is a practice of power, ruled by the powerful in society. According to the colonial/modern gender framework, history has led to a patriarchal, colonial, and capitalist society where the powerful are the men, the white, and the rich. The methodological innovation provided by Lugones (2010)'s framework applied to securitization theory allows for securitization to capture how colonial and patriarchal power dynamics are perpetuated in speech acts. Gomes and Marques (2021) argue that securitization theory can indeed save itself from sexist and racial biases if it remains unceasingly conscious of how the gender and race variables influence securitizing discourses.

1.4 Migration as a securitized issue

The securitization of migration that started in the mid-1980s continues today. Two other events reinforced and accelerated the process in recent years: 9/11 and the 2015 migration crisis. The terror attacks of September 11, 2001, were a turning point for international relations. They also had an effect on the securitization of migration both in the European Union and in the United States. Tirman (2006) finds that it revolutionized the American approach to migration, shifting the referent object of the existential threat from jobs to human lives and national sovereignty. In fact, while migration was previously considered a threat to social security, after 9/11 it became clearly linked with terrorism in the popular and political imaginary, in which "any immigrant may be a terrorist" (d'Appollonia, 2012, p. 15). On the other hand, d'Appollonia (2012) argues that the effect of the events of 9/11 on American migration policies were the same as on the EU's: it reinforced previous policies, but did not constitute "a dramatic departure" (d'Appollonia, 2012, p. 50) from them, as suggested by other readings. Karyotis (2007) also confirmed that within the European Union the 9/11 terror attacks only prompted the continuation of existing securitization trends.

Finally, the dramatic increase of refugee arrivals in the spring of 2015, with over one million refugees landing on European shores as a result of instability in other areas of the world, such as the war in Syria, has been described by scholars as a "pivotal point" (Sachseder et al., 2022, p. 1) in the process of securitization of migration. The term 'migration crisis' had been first employed in 2011 to describe new arrivals following the Arab Spring, but in 2015 it became the catchphrase politicians and journalists used to justify the securitized change in policies and narratives (Freedman, 2019).

Media discourse shifted its focus from the vulnerability of refugees facing harrowing journeys and tragedies at sea to the threat they posed to society and the limited resources of EU member states (Gray & Franck, 2019). The European Union and singular member states restricted their immigration policies, strengthened their borders, and externalized migration management through a series of agreements with third countries. These actions were justified by the explicit link policy makers drew between migration pressure and the survival of Western societies, between immigrants and crime or extremism (Sachseder et al., 2022).

Migration has not only become a securitized issue, but also a 'meta-issue', a phenomenon that can be referred to as the cause of various problems (Huysmans, 2000). Since the 1980s, in fact, the main social and security problems of Western societies, from unemployment to terrorism, have been linked to migration (Ceyhan & Tsoukala, 2002). Scholars find that discourses, or speech acts, have framed migration as an existential threat to a variety of referent objects within the nation-state. Each has been instrumental in the implementation of restrictive policies in a different area of migration governance, from integration, through displacement, to border management.

Ceyhan & Tsoukala (2002) identify four axes around which political and media narratives have defined migration as a security issue. First, the socio-economic axis linked migration to a set of social and economic problems, including unemployment and the crisis of the welfare state. Second, the securitarian axis promoted a narrative in which migration caused the loss of state control on borders and it subsequently endangered sovereignty. Third, the identitarian axis focused on the threat migrants pose to national identity and demographic equilibrium. Fourth and final, the political axis highlighted the populist advantages of anti-immigration narratives, often based on racist and xenophobic preconceptions. In summary, they find that migration "significantly affected the forms and the meanings of borders, individual and collective identities, and the sense and nature of state sovereignty and authority" (Ceyhan & Tsoukala 2002, p. 21). Similarly, d'Appollonia (2012) finds that concerns on immigration originated from its assumed negative effects on economic prosperity and social order (socio-economic axis), state sovereignty (securitarian axis), and national identity (identitarian axis).

1.5 Connecting the dots: A conceptual framework on migration, gender, and securitization

A conceptual framework is presented in order to answer the research question: *How does gender influence the securitization of migration in the European Union (EU)?* The study collocates itself among the post-colonial feminist tradition that attempts to overcome the gender-blind approach to securitization theory that has dominated within the Copenhagen School. The intrinsic nature of gender as one of the main structures that define the contemporary societal system makes it inevitable for it to influence the securitization of migration as well. However, few studies have paid attention to the specific role gender plays in influencing the success of a securitizing move. The ambivalent way refugees have been framed as both threats and referent objects, as shown in the following sections, can be explained through gender lenses: the construction of refugees as threats is based on masculinized conceptions of dangerousness, while the framing of refugees as in need of protection relies on feminized perceptions of vulnerability. I argue that an explanation for the successful securitization of migration in the EU lies in the use of gendered constructions of femininity and masculinity.

The representation of refugees in the securitization process is ambivalent. On the one hand, migrants have long been presented as existential threats to Western societies in general and the EU and its member states in particular. On the other hand, humanitarian actors, such as NGOs, have successfully framed refugees as referent objects in so-called counter-securitization moves (Massari, 2021). Besides humanitarian actors, even EU institutions and leaders' discourse has shifted from a pure securitization logic, where migrants are presented as threats, to one characterized by a humanitarian rationale, where refugees are victims to be protected by European institutions (Moreno-Lax, 2018). The European Council, during a special meeting in response to the 'migration crisis' on April 23, 2015, defined the situation a "tragedy" and declared "preventing more people from dying at sea" its priority (European Council, 2015). The tragedy consumed in the Mediterranean in 2015, with its high death tolls and images of displacement, contributed to modifying the dominant narrative into one of compassion and solidarity towards migrants.

Moreno-Lax (2018) finds that such humanitarian notions are used as justifications to advance the securitization of migration, rather than to oppose it. The language of humanitarianism is co-opted by securitizing speech acts whereby priority is posed on saving refugees as much as on protecting the EU from them. Such approach "strategically interweaves border security with human security vocabulary that helps enhance the legitimacy and reputation of securitizing forces" (Moreno-Lax, 2018, p. 6). This combined securitarian-humanitarian approach to the management of migration by the European Union relies on the construction of migration as a crisis on the basis of "a complex dynamic of threat and vulnerability" (Andersson, 2014). Discourses highlighting the threat posed by *and* to migrants co-exist and provide legitimacy to the same securitized policies.

Nevertheless, Hintjens (2019) found the framing of refugees as *at risk* to be an unsuccessful securitizing strategy for EU institutions, bound to lead to the rejection of such speech acts by the audience in light of the prior, well-established securitization of migrants as *a risk*. In fact, the current securitization of migration finds its origins in the post-Cold War era (Bello, 2022), with the labeling of migrants as threats to European cultural identity, internal security, and welfare state beginning in 2000 and becoming entrenched in the minds of public audiences (Huysmans, 2000). However, the catastrophic events of 2015 caused a shift in the dominant discourse and the humanitarian narrative of the crisis conquered, for some time, the hearts and minds of the audience. European institutions and policy-makers joined in on the message that in order to protect migrants from the deathly effects of illegal migration extraordinary measures had to be adopted.

This monograph argues that introducing gender and taking into account how gendered constructions influence securitization might counter Hintjens (2019)'s finding that framing refugees as referent objects results in a failed securitizing move. While it is recognized that the securitization of migrants had been well underway before and during 2015, the idea of refugees as referent objects is not as novel, especially when *female* refugees are considered, and neither is their association with the figure of the 'good migrant' in the eyes of the audience. The theme of vulnerable women as "at risk" has been central to the construction of migration as a crisis (Gray & Franck, 2019; Sachseder et al., 2022; Schrover, 2019), as shown in the following section. The logics of vulnerable femininity are "familiar rather than foreign to the designated audience" (Gray & Franck, 2019, p. 276), in a society where the main social structures are constructed on the basis of gendered and racialized assumptions established long before the current securitization of migration even took place. Audiences reason on the basis of "ordinary ideas about vulnerability and threat [that] ground dominant ways of understanding the world" (Gray & Franck, 2019, p. 286). Such ideas reflect the patriarchal binary of masculinity and femininity in the EU's securitarian-humanitarian approach to migration management.

1.6 Gender (and race) in securitization and crisis labeling

The introduction of gender into the securitization framework of migration aims to address the critique of gender-blindness towards the Copenhagen School and to find whether gender plays a specific role in the successful securitization of migration. Previous research by Gray and Franck (2019) has argued that "securitizing moves are made possible by intertwined and mutually dependent gendered and racialized representations of refugee threat *and* vulnerability". Their analysis of speech acts in the British media found that throughout time the notions of masculinized threat and gendered vulnerability have functioned as co-existing categories in securitizing frames. Moffette and Vadasaria (2016) similarly demonstrate that securitization is also a gendered and racialized process. Additional empirical studies are needed in order to investigate how gender influences the success of securitization.

Most of the existing research has focused on how gendered stereotypes support the construction of migration as a crisis (Gray & Franck, 2019; Sachseder et al., 2022; Schrover, 2019). Crisis labeling can be considered as a step in securitization theory. It is the construction of a 'crisis' "as a reality distinguishable from the 'normal'" (Sachseder et al., 2022, p. 6), which provides the sense of urgency and justification to frame an issue as an existential threat. Crisis labeling is part of the securitizing move, and it is provoked by the challenging event that sets in motion the securitization process. Global migration crises, for example, are "socially constructed scattered inflamed reactions that have been happening since the end of Cold War, as a consequence of forced movements of people" (Bello, 2022, p. 1327).

The emigration of people because of growing instability in different areas of the world has caused elites to invoke the idea of a migration crisis, legitimizing framing the issue as an existential threat. Scholars found that crisis as a social construct is structured by "socio-economic and political inequalities and unequal power relations" (Sachseder et al., 2022, p. 6), based on intersectional gendered, racial, and class marginalization. Sachseder et al. (2022) discovered that gendered and racial stereotypes were used to provide legitimacy to the construction of the migration crisis in the European Union developing around four themes: the 'unknownness' of migrants; migration as a threat; humanitarian concerns over vulnerable migrants; the hierarchical creation of (non-) European spaces.

Firstly, the 'unknownness of migrants' theme relies on the underpinned notions of migrants as "unknown", "unpredictable", and "deceiving". The lack of knowledge of and unfamiliarity with the cultural identities of immigrants by the host community leads to a process of 'othering', where not only are the 'others' different but it is also unknown in which ways they differ; it is much more dangerous, especially amidst the identity crisis that Western societies have been experiencing. Luthman (2017) uses Jacque Derrida's paradox of hospitality to explain the concept. On the one hand, hospitality, as conceptualized by the Ancient Greek notion of *xenia*, is conditional: a host welcomes a guest with shelter and protection in order to gain the favor of Zeus *Xenios*. On the other hand, hospitality requires the host to welcome in their safe space an "absolute, unknown, anonymous other" (Derrida, 2000, p. 25), giving up control and the ability to determine who the guest is and whether they pose a threat. This leads the host to assume that the guest is "wrong, illegitimate, clandestine" (Luthman, 2017, p. 12). In summary, the unknown and assumed threatening character of the 'foreign other' is used to legitimize the securitization of migrants.

Secondly, a key theme at the basis of crisis labeling and securitization is the framing of migration as a dual threat. Political and media discourses – either pro or anti – only see migration in terms of the problems it poses: anti-immigration proponents focus on the challenges a society or government has to face because of immigrants, from provision of housing for new arrivals to their absorption into the labor force; pro-migration narratives emphasize the obstacles migrants have to face throughout their journeys, as well as during and after arrival. Migration is framed as a threat to both the host society and to migrants themselves. While supporters or opponents of migration pick and choose the relevant referent object, the binary construction of migration as a threat originates from gendered stereotypes and not from differing political views. It is based on the "intertwined and mutually dependent representations of masculinized threat and feminized vulnerability" (Gray & Franck, 2019, p. 276).

Gender is the defining characteristic that differentiates between racialized migrants being a risk to a society's labor market and security, or at risk of being victims of human trafficking, gender-based violence, or culture-specific issues (Schrover, 2019). The securitization of female migration is based on a different assumption of that of male migration. On the one hand, migrant men, especially if non-Western, able-bodied, and single, are framed as threatening. On the other, migrant racialized women are represented as particularly vulnerable and in need of protection. The constant and dominant narrative of migrant women's exclusive helplessness has had negative effects on both migrant men and women. It has taken away agency from women and silenced their voices (Freedman, 2019) and it has invisibilized migrant men's own vulnerabilities in times when they are also facing extremely insecure situations, such as war and dangerous journeys.

Thirdly, the vulnerability discourse is used to advance humanitarian concerns that legitimize the labeling of migration as a crisis. Once again, the process is based on patriarchal and colonial archetypes, with gender and race determining "who is deemed worthy of protection and who is seen as an able trustworthy protector" (Sachseder et al., 2022, p. 7). The former are racialized migrant women at all stages of the migratory journey, the latter are Western men and women in the countries of arrival. The supposed vulnerability of women has been used even by pro-migration advocates among policy-makers and NGOs to create a sense of urgency to the issue and generate empathy among the audience, ultimately framing migration as a crisis in order to advance the cause of humanitarian support to migrants. For example, campaigns that employ images of refugee women and children in transit camps have been successful in raising funds and awareness (Freedman, 2010).

While at times migrant women themselves benefit from their representation as vulnerable – another example is the strategic use of perceived vulnerability by women travelling alone and ahead of their families to readily gain asylum status (Freedman, 2019) – the concept always has negative connotations. Being vulnerable is equated with being incapable of protecting oneself and others and instead needing protection. This notion robs migrant women of agency, subjecting them to the decisions of those who self-appointed themselves as the 'protectors' (Schrover, 2019). Migrant women's voices are silenced, their needs and wishes are never communicated firsthand but through the interpretation of, possibly good willing, organizations and practitioners. In securitization theory, actors who are constrained in their ability to perform a speech act are prevented from becoming "subjects worthy of consideration and protection" (Freedman, 2010, p. 604).

Refugee women thus are unable to contribute to the securitization of migration on the basis of what they deem to be an existential threat, which will undoubtedly differ from the view of Western elites. Securitized migration policies will perpetuate patriarchal and colonial practices as long as they exclude the voices of women from the Global South. Furthermore, the fact that some migrant women can indeed be vulnerable does not mean that all female migrants are. The homogenization of all migrant women in a monolithic group, often joined with the other vulnerable categories of children and elders and where women are primarily mothers protecting their children, depoliticizes the struggle of women and erases the historical and social causes of intersectional marginalization (Morán & Teano, 2020).

Fourthly, the vulnerability narrative is also supported by post-colonial gendered and racial hierarchies. The hierarchical creation of (non-)European spaces furthers the 'othering' process according to colonial stereotypes: 'foreign others' are placed underneath the West in a hierarchy of cultures; they are often deemed to be culturally backwards in respect to the self-representation of the Western gold standard of a developed society. Hierarchies are both racialized and gendered (Sachseder et al., 2022). As first theorized by Mohanty (1984), depictions of the 'Third World woman' are the product of a post-colonial, patriarchal system that combines stereotypes on gender and race to create a monolithic image of racialized women as victims of their own 'backwards' cultures.

Morán and Teano (2020) illustrate that in the narrative of European elites, racialized women are "mere faces without voice, bodies without their own agency" (p. 124). Such a view contributes to the 'othering' process even within the social category of women, reinforcing the alleged differences and the subsequent disconnection between Western and non-Western women. (Freedman, 2010). Discourses based on such stereotypes tend to fixate on issues that women do face but that are exclusively related to non-Western customs, leading to hyper-visibility of matters such as trafficking, forced marriages, and even the wearing of hijabs. At the same time, issues that originate from social inequalities that affect women transnationally are rendered invisible.

The second and third themes are of particular relevance for the research. The depiction of migration as a crisis relies on assumptions of feminized vulnerability and masculinized threat in order to advance the securitization process and selects the one which will sustain the dominating narrative in response to the development of events, in order to successfully convince the audience of the presence of an existential threat and of the need to mobilize extraordinary resources. For example, while media discourse in the early months of 2015 focused on feminized vulnerability of refugees escaping war and facing the journey to Europe, the terror attack in Paris in November 2015 caused the media to shift their narrative to one of masculinized threat, emboldened by the male identity of the terrorists (Gray & Franck, 2019). Migrants were thus converged into a monolithic group posing a threat to Europe. Furthermore, the gendered aspect of the vulnerability discourse complements the finding by Moreno-Lax (2018), according to whom humanitarian narratives legitimize the securitization of migration.

In conclusion, the findings from previous literature contribute to the development of a theoretical framework on migration, gender, and securitization. Scholars have found that the dual securitarian-humanitarian approach of the EU towards migration management, justifying the activation of extraordinary, military resources, is based on the dual framing of migrants as both a threat and a referent object. Whether they are categorized as one or the other depends on, among other factors such as race, the gendered assumptions constituting the patriarchal system in which migration takes place. The monograph aims to addresses specific knowledge gaps in the literature on a topic that has not been extensively explored to date by investigating how such gendered frames of threat and vulnerability are utilized in order to legitimize the securitization of migration in the EU.

1.7 Gender in EU migration policies

The present section aims to review the literature on the role of gender in the specific securitization of EU migration policies. Few studies have addressed how gender contributes to the construction of securitized policies on migration management. In particular, this paper wants to fill the knowledge gap identified by Sachseder et al. (2022) regarding which "gendered (and racialized) crisis narratives are institutionally anchored and inscribed into the practices of the emerging EU border security architecture" (p. 6). Applying the conceptual framework previously introduced at the European level allows to set the expectation that the gendered constructions of 'feminine' vulnerability and 'masculine' threat are among the security frames underpinning the securitization of migration policies in the EU.

Sachseder et al. (2022), in their gender-based analysis of the securitization of Frontex, found that ideas of masculinity and dangerousness, as well as of femininity and vulnerability, are embedded within the Agency's institutional framework and have provided the justification for its expansion and militarization. Specifically, Frontex itself relies on and reproduces gendered stereotypes in order to construct migration as a crisis and guarantee not only its survival but also its prosperity. The post-colonial feminist interpretation of crisis labeling that focuses on its gendered foundations allows linking "gendered crisis constructions that normalize emergency measures to the trajectories of institutions designed to identify and handle such crisis politically and practically" (Sachseder et al., 2022a, p. 19). The reproduction of systems of meaning based on gender stereotypes within the Agency as well as within the broader European border security architecture legitimizes the narrative of migration as a crisis and contributes to the institutionalization of the securitization of migration in the EU.

In such a process of crisis labeling, migrants have been alternately masculinized and feminized for more than a decade. On the one hand, the representation of refugees as dangerous, unknown, foreign, and threatening, either posing a risk to European citizens or wanting to exploit member states' welfare systems, primarily engages the figure of the male migrant. It is based on constructions of (racialized) masculinity, whose characteristics are transferred to migrant women when the securitizing actor – here Frontex – deems fit. On the other hand, "feminization and victimization of migrants in the context of masculinist protectionism and white saviorism" (Sachseder et al., 2022, p. 7) have been crucial in legitimizing the migrant crisis discourse. The "white men saving brown women from brown men" (Spivak, 1988) postulate resonates with the self-referencing of Frontex as a rescuer and of migrants as referent objects. In this context, it is not only migrant women who adhere to socially constructed ideas of femininity, but the whole migrant population is feminized as vulnerable and in need of protection.

Beyond Frontex, the role of gender in EU-wide policy responses to the 2015 migration crisis has been analyzed by Welfens (2020). The scholar explores how gendered constructions influence "problem representations and proposed solutions" (Welfens, 2020, p. 514) in the EU Agenda on Migration. She found that internal responses to the crisis, such as the Common European Asylum System (CEAS), focus on "protecting refugees inside", with vulnerable migrants becoming the referent objects and their protection needs carefully and comprehensively considered through a gender lens. On the contrary, external European responses to the crisis, including all migration-related responses in third countries or international waters, focus on "protecting borders abroad". The vulnerability of migrants is essentialized to the notion of "womenandchildren" (Enloe, 1990), and it becomes a tool for restricting migration, as also conceptualized by Moreno-Lax (2018)'s securitarian-humanitarian nexus. Vulnerability is thus a concept that is worth exploring in depth.

Vulnerability in EU migration management architecture

Vulnerability has become the new popular "buzzword" in the EU fora, where migration policy is discussed (Hruschka & Leboeuf, 2019). Since the 2015 migration crisis, the record number of arrivals and overwhelming requests for asylum have shaped asylum policies around a "vulnerability contest" (Turner, 2021, p. 1) to determine who is "a 'good' refugee worthy of support" and who are "the 'bad' migrants [...] seeking to abuse the system to gain protection which they do not deserve" (Freedman, 2019b, p. 2). The term originated outside of the realm of international relations; it was borrowed by feminist scholars from environmental studies in the 1980s, describing the impact of natural disasters on humans. The feminist conception of vulnerability has two iterations. Firstly, vulnerability is universal; in line with the original conception, being vulnerable is considered inherently human: all humans are vulnerable. Secondly, vulnerability is context-dependent and relational; political and social conditions may cause vulnerability to be unequally distributed among groups, with some becoming more vulnerable than others (Turner, 2021).

Feminist research has demonstrated that constructions of vulnerability and protection are highly gendered (Welfens, 2020). The policies that the

EU has created to manage migration exacerbate the gendered vulnerabilities experienced by migrants (Freedman, 2019). The assumption that "womenand-children" (Enloe, 1990) are the most vulnerable group among migrants is long-standing and widely shared, reinforced by racialized perceptions of the "Third World woman" (Mohanty, 1984). While recognizing a special vulnerable status can have strategic advantages in various phases of the migratory process, it poses different problems for both those identified as such and those excluded from such categorization.

A group approach to vulnerability identifies those who are vulnerable on the basis of pre-determined categorization. The approach has both inclusionary and exclusionary consequences. The assumption that certain migrants are vulnerable *a priori* because of their belonging to a group that legislative documents classify as vulnerable generalizes and essentializes the protection needs of individuals without taking into account their personal lived experiences and disregarding any agency they might have in expressing their needs. Furthermore, the approach produces a "hidden exclusionary effect" (Hruschka & Leboeuf, 2019). Groups that are framed as non- or less- vulnerable are excluded from accessing certain rights deemed exclusive to vulnerable persons, for example, receiving asylum status (Hruschka & Leboeuf, 2019).

International organizations, including the EU, employ a group approach to define who is vulnerable and worthy of protection. The EU has increasingly included the notion of vulnerability, although failing to develop a coherent definition, in response to critiques of gender-blindness in its migration policies. Thus, the concept, as presented in the European framework, is highly gendered. It first appeared in Article 21 of Directive 2013/33/EU6, where numerous categories of migrants were deemed "vulnerable", including pregnant women, women victims of trafficking, and women victims of sexual violence.

Welfens (2020) found that comprehensive understandings of gendered vulnerabilities were integrated into the internal policies of the CEAS. The 2011 Qualifications Directive obliges member states to consider the "specific situation of vulnerable persons such as victims of human trafficking [...] and persons who have been subjected to rape or other serious forms of psychological, physical or sexual violence" (European Parliament, 2011). The 2013 recast Reception Directive identifies vulnerable persons to include "(unaccompanied) minors, disabled people, elderly people, pregnant women, single parents with minor children, victims of human trafficking, persons with serious illnesses or mental disorders, and persons who have been subjugated to torture, rape or other serious forms of psychological, physical or sexual violence, such as victims of female genital mutilation" (European Parliament, 2013).

The discourse on vulnerability in internal policy documents does not employ a women-centric approach but rather an intersectional gender-centric one. Gender is one of the social markers that, in interaction with others, such as health, conjugal status, and age, constitutes grounds for receiving special status as vulnerable and access to the rights associated with the categorization. On the contrary, EU external policies are riddled with essentializing pitfalls of group vulnerability. The language is the simplistic one of "womenand-children" (Enloe, 1990).

The current conceptualization and integration of vulnerability in the EU migration policy, especially in externally-oriented solutions, "carries a real risk of essentialization of women as vulnerable victims and on the contrary of a denial of men's possible vulnerability as they are perceived only as a threat or danger" (Freedman, 2019b, p. 12). However, the vulnerability of migrant men is being increasingly recognized and academic research on the subject is growing (Allsopp, 2017; El-Bushra & Gardner, 2016; Turner, 2021, 2016). Paradoxically, vulnerability is both a constituting factor and an effect of EU policies.

The securitization of EU policies has exacerbated the vulnerability of all refugees by pushing them to take additional risks in order to reach Europe (Freedman, 2019b). The conclusion that the inclusionary and exclusionary effects of vulnerability are gendered confirms the expectations put forward by this monograph: gendered vulnerabilities, with women being presented as vulnerable and men as threatening, lie at the heart of the securitization of EU migration management. The following section focuses on the exclusionary character of vulnerability and the particular framing of migrant men.

Masculinized threat in EU migration management architecture

It is now apparent how a gendered understanding of vulnerability often risks being, or is, synonymous with women's vulnerability in EU external policies. This tendency also exists in academia, with scholars using 'gender' as a substitute for 'women'. In general, literature linking masculinity and migration is scarce, and the study of the "discursive construction of migrant masculinity has to date rarely been done" (Wyss, 2022, p. 73). This monograph aims to address such a knowledge gap by analyzing the specific role gender, including masculinity, has in framing migrants as threats in EU policies. Wyss (2022) found that representations of migrant men as dangerous and criminal justify and legitimize the securitization of the EU's migration governance. Her analysis of the practical implementation of the EU's migration legislation reveals that it "relies strongly on gendered and racialized assessments of deservingness" (Wyss, 2022, p. 73), where vulnerable femininities are deserving and threatening masculinities are not.

The vulnerability discourse in the securitization of migration at the EU level creates a dichotomy between 'good' and 'bad' migrants, one to be saved and the other to be saved from. The distinction between migrants un- or deserving to be rescued, recognized legal status, and integrated into European society is thus based on grounds of vulnerability (Wyss, 2022), which, as the previous section made apparent, is gendered. The vulnerability discourse differentiates between men and women, with "gender, implicitly or explicitly, drawing the boundaries between wanted and unwanted migration" (Welfens, 2020, p. 512). This conception of gendered vulnerability influences the securitization process. While vulnerable groups, often women and children, are framed as referent objects to be protected in various EU policies, migrant men become the threats to be protected from. As summarized by de Norohna (2015), "in general, the 'bad migrant' is a man" (p. 9). Racialized male migrants are essentialized into the figure of the "undeserving 'other'" (Wyss, 2022, p. 53), framed as either 'bogus' asylum seekers or economic migrants seeking to exploit the EU's system.

In addition to features of 'undeservigness', the securitization of migrant men relies on the inherently violent character attributed to (racialized) masculinities. The framing of men, especially young, heterosexual, and single ones who are not categorized into vulnerable groups, as intrinsically dangerous relies on a long-standing "unquestioned assumption" (Pruitt et al., 2018, p. 699) that "[young] men are always potentially dangerous, morally deviant and sexually violent" (de Norohna, 2015, p. 13). Migrant men thus pose not only a socio-economic and identitarian threat to the EU but also a securitarian threat to European citizens (Ceyhan & Tsoukala, 2002).

The criminal-migrant thesis, according to which migrants engage in criminal activities throughout the EU after accessing the Schengen area, is also gendered: both figures of the 'bad migrant' and the 'criminal' are generally assumed to be male (de Norohna, 2015). Feminist literature identified this assumption as a central trope in portrayals of migrant men throughout time. For example, de Norohna (2015)'s analysis of public discourse during the 2006 Foreign National Prisoner crisis in the UK found it to be characterized by a gendered victim-villain binary, where the former were often women and the latter men. However, in the context of the migration crisis, representations of this kind have multiplied and assumed a central role in the securitization process.

Previous research has explored how these representations grounded speech acts by one particular securitizing agent, the media. They were first utilized after the terror attacks in Paris on 13 November 2015, when media narrative shifted from that of the vulnerable refugee that characterized the first phase of the migration crisis. Newspaper articles created a divide between vulnerable feminized migrants and dangerous masculinized incomers, epitomized in the Bataclan male terrorists (Gray & Franck, 2019). Further securitization of migrant men was prompted by a challenging event that led to the resurgence of frames of migrant men as dangerous and criminal: at the end of 2015, numerous incidents of mass sexual harassment were perpetuated by migrant men in Cologne as well as other Northern European cities. Gray and Franck (2019)'s analysis of British newspapers found that the event inspired the explicit gendering of narratives in the media that clearly labeled young, single migrant men as threats to European women and gender equality at large.

Similarly, Pruitt et al. (2018) found that media reports emphasized the gendered male appearance of the perpetrators and their categorization as migrants in order to legitimize the perceived threat posed by migrant men. Wyss (2022) analyzed how the events that took place in Cologne during the 2016 New Year festivities were instrumentalized by public and political discourse in order to legitimize the securitization of migration and advocate for more restrictive policies. The assailants, who were reportedly described as "North African-looking men" (Yurdakul & Korteweg, 2021), came to epitomize all racialized migrant men.

The gravity of the act, especially given the EU's self-representation as a champion of gender equality and a safe space for women (Welfens, 2020), led to the demonization of the figure of the migrant man as a dangerous sexual predator, which, with its appeal to strong emotions and to masculinized protection of European women, underscored successful speech acts arguing for the adoption of a securitized approach to migration management. A similar strategy was adopted in Austria in the summer of 2015 when foreign masculinity was framed by the political leadership in such a way as to "delegitimize solidarity with them and to argue for restrictive measures" (Scheibelhofer, 2017, p. 96). The negative portrayal of migrant men was crucial in establishing a securitizing perspective on migration management in Austria.

Much of the research thus far has focused on the negative framing of migrant men in public discourse through the analysis of media articles (de Norohna, 2015; Gray & Franck, 2019; Pruitt et al., 2018; Scheibelhofer, 2017; Wyss, 2022) and even press releases by NGOs (de Norohna, 2015) or political parties (Scheibelhofer, 2017). On the contrary, the employment of such a security frame in EU policies remains understudied. It is important to note that political, public, and legal narratives interweave in a mutually reinforcing process where one influences the other and vice versa. It is, therefore, reasonable to expect that the representation of migrants as a threat on the basis of masculinized stereotypes of aggressiveness, dangerousness, and 'undeservigness', which, as shown by the paragraphs above, exist in public discourse, is reproduced in EU political narratives and policy documents. A specific study that investigates how the gendered binary underpins the securitized policies of an EU migration agency is Stachowitsch and Sachseder (2019)'s analysis of the narrative contents of Frontex's risk analysis.

Stachowitsch and Sachseder (2019) applied frame analysis to Frontex's Annual Risk Analysis Report (RAR), an intelligence dissemination product that is the centerpiece of the Agency's risk analysis publications. The authors identify three security frames in the 2016 document that were used to justify the controversial restrictive border control measures Frontex carried out following the 2015 migration crisis. Each was based on masculinized constructions of threats to the EU. Firstly, the 'pressure' frame stemmed from the "unprecedented" number of migrants that arrived on European shores in 2015. In the RAR, the crowds were portrayed as unmanageable not only because of their size but because of the risks posed by "single men with different backgrounds and nationalities" (Frontex, 2016, p. 45). The 'othering' process that argued that Third World migrants' inability to integrate into Western societies made them particularly hard to manage assumed a gendered dimension. The RAR suggests that migrants violate Western gender norms when they supposedly "endanger their women" (Stachowitsch & Sachseder, 2019, p. 114) during the journey or because of culture-specific customs.

In general, masculinities were problematized in the document through an inherent link to potentially aggressive and violent behavior, which was presented as one of the main difficulties in the member states and their law enforcement's management of migrant crowds. The representation of masculinity in the document is based on a narrow and limited understanding of men's experiences. Migrant men have been typified as either "battle-hardened jihadists [with] atrocious *modi operandi*" or smugglers "whose ruthlessness has resulted in a number of maritime tragedies" (Frontex, 2016, p. 39). The hypermasculinization of migrant men presents them as a serious threat to the EU and justifies the employment of extraordinary measures by Frontex to fight terrorists and smugglers. These are naturally accepted by the audience in light of the existential fear the former evokes and the continuous sole blame attributed to the latter for the en masse arrival of migrants by EU politicians. The findings by Stachowitsch and Sachseder (2019) introduce the gendered dimension of the masculinized threat in Ceyhan and Tsoukala (2002)'s securitarian axis of the securitization of migration.

The second frame lies alongside the socio-economic axis: 'economic migrants' are framed as posing a threat to societies in the EU by consuming resources reserved for local citizens and disrupting the job market. The framing of the migrant as an "immoral *homo oeconomicus*" (Stachowitsch & Sachseder, 2019, p. 116) who is undeserving of a place in European societies, with all the social and economic benefits associated with it, recurs in the narrative perpetuated by Frontex. In the RAR, the concept assumes a clearly gendered dimension where economic migrants are primarily described as "young men who are pushed by economic motivations" (Frontex, 2016, p. 45) and "take advantage of the situation" (p. 8). Thus, the immorality of the character of the economic migrant is underpinned by stereotypes of masculinity which portray men as risky and undeserving of support. Additionally, their portrayal as a danger to the welfare system of EU member states legitimizes Frontex's practices of returns of economic migrants to their country of origin or to the previous transit country. Stachowitsch and Sachseder (2019) found that "the system of returns requires masculinization to portray the economic migrant as a threat" (p. 117).

Finally, the third frame identified in the document relies on humanitarianism to advance Frontex's securitized policies and practices. As previously discussed, the co-optation of humanitarian language is a specific strategy employed by EU securitizing actors that combines discourse on protecting and protection, on vulnerability and threat (Moreno-Lax, 2018). Consequently, the humanitarian frame "produces particular lives that are worthy of being saved or sacrificed" (Pallister-Wilkins, 2015). The two are differentiated according to gender: while women and other vulnerable groups are framed as referent objects in light of their feminized vulnerability, men are not only excluded from such categorization but often become the threat the referent object needs to be protected from. While in the two previous frames, migrant men threatened the EU's sovereignty, security, or internal market, in the third, the "ruthless" (Frontex, 2016, p. 18) violent male migrant or smuggler endangers his fellow migrant women. The RAR reports that "the crowds also mixed young single men with more vulnerable families, including women and children, sometimes purposely put in front of the groups to facilitate their progression" (Frontex, 2016, p. 45).

While a majority of existing research has traced the employment of the feminized vulnerability and masculinized threat frames in public discourse and, in particular, in the media, less attention has been dedicated to the speech acts performed by EU institutions in the form of policy or legislative documents. The few studies that address the topic focus on border control and Frontex's risk analysis (Sachseder et al., 2022; Stachowitsch & Sachseder, 2019), with the notable exception of Welfens (2020)'s analysis of the EU Agenda on Migration. The monograph aims to fill the knowledge gap by exploring the gendered underpinnings of a major border control policy of the EU that, despite its centrality in the migration management framework, has not been studied so far: the anti-smuggling and anti-trafficking regimes.

Methodology

2.1 Critical Frame Analysis

One of the principal criticisms moved to the original iteration of securitization theory is its over-reliance on the speech act as the actualization of the securitizing move. The feminist critique of the Copenhagen School – of particular importance for this monograph – considers the speech act framework's inability to take into account the gendered power dynamics in situations when speech is not possible (Howell & Richter-Montpetit, 2020). The critical role that discourses and narratives have in securitization theory, in which utterances are powerful enough to turn a politicized issue into a securitized one, poses a problem in cases where the ability of an actor to perform a speech act is constrained or non-existent. Actors who are unable to voice their insecurity are prevented from becoming "subjects worthy of consideration and protection", and their issues will never be included in the security agenda as long as they remain "silent security problems" (Hansen, 2000, p. 285).

In order to overcome the limitations of the speech act-centered approach, Stępka (2022) proposed to interpret securitization "as the work of framing" (p. 34). Framing is a process in which some aspects of an issue are made "more salient in a communicating text, in such a way as to promote a particular problem definition, causal interpretation, moral evaluation, and/or treatment recommendation" (Entman, 1993, p. 52). It not only identifies what the problem – in the case of securitization, the threat – is, but it also considers what solution – in the case of securitization, which extraordinary measure – is proposed. This process does not simply occur in one single speech act that

speaks the threat into existence. Instead, it is the product of multiple iterations of the issue in public and political speeches, media articles and video
news, policy directives, and legislative regulations. Repetition is the key to
normalizing the message in the minds of the audience as the acceptable way
of 'thinking and doing' about an issue. As a result, the audience will be more
likely to accept the securitizing move.

Framing has been employed in various fields, such as media and communications, social movement research, and policy studies. The application of the
latter is particularly relevant to this research and to its analysis of directives
and other policy documents on anti-smuggling and anti-trafficking. It has
been shown that policy framing can contribute to the study of securitization
since "by substituting speech acts with framing, securitization assumes a
more nuanced character" (Stępka, 2022, p. 37). Rather than relying on the
explicit statement of the threat in a single 'decisive' speech act, securitization
of an issue can be more subtly spotted through a dynamic, layered reading
of policies. The analysis needs to go beyond what is simply stated in the
policy, which is the reflection of an actor's both 'discursive' and 'practical'
consciousness (Verloo & Lombardo, 2007). The former refers to the message
the actor intends to communicate, while the latter concerns the prejudices
that are associated with the message and that the actor unknowingly per-
petuates in the policy.

Prejudices are conceptualized according to the Gadamerian interpretation of "socially constructed and cultural filters through which we perceive,
understand, and give meaning to reality" (Verloo & Lombardo, 2007, p. 32).
As patriarchal and racial systems of meaning dominate our understanding
of the world, scholars found that "actors may provide a representation of a
given policy problem that is more gender-, or race-biased than they actually
wished" (Verloo & Lombardo, 2007, p. 32). Framing is deemed to be the
most suitable methodology for this monograph because of its potential for
the analysis of both securitization (Stępka, 2022) and gender issues (Verloo
& Lombardo, 2007) since the aim of this research project is to understand
how gendered notions contribute to the process of securitization of EU
migration policies. Gender prejudices of what it means to be a man and
what it means to be a woman, of femininity and masculinity, transpire in
the representation of who is dangerous and a threat and who is vulnerable
and a referent object.

In order to reveal "what is actually hidden under the carpet?" (Verloo & Lombardo, 2007, p. 41) in EU policies on smuggling and trafficking in terms of gendered stereotypes, Critical Frame Analysis is employed. Critical Frame Analysis is a feminist adaptation of frame analysis, a research method developed by the sociologist Erving Goffman to investigate the socially-constructed frames individuals employ to interpret social interactions (Goffman, 1974). Since its first inception, frame analysis has evolved and has been applied to a variety of fields, from communications studies to political science. In the early 2000s, scholars involved in the European Commission-funded MAGEEQ project on gender mainstreaming developed a multi-disciplinary variation of the methodology on the basis of theoretical notions from social movement theory, public policy, and gender theory (Peace Institute, 2003). Welfens (2020) finds that such an approach is "well suited to analyze gender consideration in EU policies" (p. 514). This is because, through Critical Frame Analysis, it is possible to "grasp the nuances of a policy frame" (Verloo & Lombardo, 2007, p. 37).

A mixed-method approach to Critical Frame Analysis is employed in this research, which utilizes deductive and inductive coding (Semetko & Valkenburg, 2000). The analysis of the policies defining the EU anti-trafficking and anti-smuggling regimes will be guided, similarly to Verloo's (2005) and Welfens' (2020), by a set of synthetizing questions on the basis of the findings from previous literature. Since the research is interested in the securitization of such policies, the dimensions that are most relevant are the diagnosis of the problem, ergo, how the issue is constructed as a threat, and the prognosis, meaning which extraordinary measures are employed. In particular, the roles of different actors highlighted within the framing of the issue are explored: who is responsible for the problem, whom does the problem affect, and who are possible victims and perpetrators? (Verloo & Roggeband, 2007). Using the software MAXQDA to conduct a qualitative content analysis, the selected policy documents on smuggling and trafficking are examined in order to identify major themes sustaining the two primary frames.

An initial list of codes (see Appendix A) has been deductively compiled based on the previous findings highlighted in the literature review. Thereafter, during the analysis, an additional arch-frame was inductively identified and added to the codebook. The main aim of the analysis is to identify how frames of masculinized threat and feminized vulnerability in the diagnosis of the problems of smuggling and trafficking have led to a prognosis based on securitization of the issues and the mobilization of extraordinary resources to deal with them. Thus, the investigation through Critical Frame Analysis focuses on both the diagnosis and the prognosis. Two different codebooks have been compiled for the two dimensions: in the diagnosis, the so-called 'arch-frames', the primary narratives in the three-level structure of the analysis, are masculinized threat and feminized vulnerability. Within the arch-frames, regular frames and subframes further specify the way the problem is presented. Ten frames and seven subframes have been extracted from the literature as relevant to the construction of the two arch-frames. Regarding feminized vulnerability, these are: 'unaware & disinformed victims'; 'deserving migrant'; 'womenandchildren'; 'sexual exploitation'; 'abuse & gender-based violence'.

While the arch-frame of feminized vulnerability relies on the explicit reference to the specific vulnerability of women, some of the other frames implicitly relate to femininity, as elaborated by different authors. The connection to vulnerable femininity is clear in the cases of the frames of 'womenandchildren', 'sexual exploitation', and 'abuse and gender-based violence'. Women are essentialized and infantilized when grouped in a single vulnerable category alongside minors (Welfens, 2020). Empirically, women are more likely to be victims of sexual exploitation and abuse and gender-based violence, and the concepts have become primarily associated with vulnerabilities specific to women and girls, although men and boys can also be affected. Stachowitsch and Sachseder (2019) found that being irrational and more prone to be victim to disinformation has been stereotyped as a trait of female migrants. Furthermore, the specific gendered vulnerabilities identified above, among others, contribute to the idea of women as winners of the "vulnerability contest" (Turner, 2021, p. 1) and, therefore, as 'deserving migrants' who get to integrate into European society, receive its protection, and access its benefits (Freedman, 2019; Wyss, 2022).

The frames that contribute to the representation of feminized vulnerability also affect the creation of frames within the arch-frame of masculinized threat. The categorization of who is vulnerable produces a "hidden exclusionary effect" (Hruschka & Leboeuf, 2019), whereby others are excluded from the benefits and protection that comes with the label. When certain groups are explicitly identified as vulnerable, others are implicitly excluded from such a definition. Furthermore, while women are usually characterized as deserving, men are usually considered as 'undeserving migrants'. They are portrayed as 'bad', denied their legal right to migration, and even declared "worthy of being sacrificed" (Pallister-Wilkins, 2015). The 'undeservingness' of male migrants is motivated on the basis of the assumptions developed along Ceyhan and Tsoukala (2002)'s axes. Each axis, securitarian, socio-economic, and identitarian, is a frame that becomes operationalized by a number of subframes. The identitarian frame considers the threat migrants supposedly pose to the EU through the 'pressure' subframe. Stachowitsch and Sachseder (2019) found that the pressure of increasing migratory flows had distressed the EU not only because of the extreme burden on the migration management infrastructures, but also because of the alien nature of the foreign 'other', especially when he was a man.

The securitarian frame concerns the threat to the safety, security, and stability of the referent object. It is operationalized through four subframes that concern both the figure of the migrant man and of the smuggler or trafficker. Firstly, they are assumed to engage in criminal behavior. While this is self-explanatory for smugglers and traffickers, as their business is criminality, for migrants, the explanation relies on the criminal-migrant monograph. Feminist literature has confirmed the prejudice connecting criminality to masculinity (de Norohna, 2015). Related to criminal behavior, in the subframe of 'violence' and 'sexual predators, ' migrants, smugglers, and traffickers are essentialized to "potentially dangerous, morally deviant and sexually violent" (de Norohna, 2015, p. 13) men. The socio-economic frame is operationalized differently according to the actor. The migrant is portrayed as an "immoral homo oeconomicus" (Stachowitsch & Sachseder, 2019, p. 116) who becomes a threat to the EU's labor market and welfare system. The connection to masculinity in this case is sustained by long-standing stereotypes of men as the breadwinners who migrate in order to provide for their 'foreign' families at the expense of European workers (Guild et al., 2016; Stachowitsch & Sachseder, 2019). Smugglers and traffickers are also moved by short-term and long-term profit.

The second codebook refers to the prognosis proposed by the policy documents. The diagnosis highlights how an issue comes to pose an existential threat. In the prognosis, a possible way out is presented through the proposal of employing extraordinary measures, including the legitimate use of force. Thus, securitization is the arch-frame that governs the prognosis dimension of a policy document. The frames are the elements comprising the securitization process: 'securitized threat'; 'referent object'; 'extraordinary measures'; 'ordinary measures'. The same securitized policies are legitimized by co-existing subframes of the threat posed by and to migrants. On the one hand, the humanitarian approach to smuggling and trafficking identifies them as threats to migrants. On the other hand, the securitarian approach focuses on the threats smuggling and trafficking pose to the EU. Critical Frame Analysis allows one to dig deeper into the documents beyond what is simply stated or not stated. By identifying the selected frames that have been employed to define masculinity and femininity in previous work, it is possible to trace whether the conceptions of threat and vulnerability are constructed on the basis of gendered prejudices.

2.2 Document Selection

Seven policy documents were selected for analysis among the policy documents identified by the literature review on anti-smuggling and anti-trafficking governance in the previous chapter. In regard to the analysis of the anti-smuggling regime, its major policies were identified: EU Action Plan against Migrant Smuggling (2015–2020); 2017 REFIT evaluation of the EU legal framework against facilitation of unauthorized entry, transit and residence: the Facilitators Package; A renewed EU Action Plan against Migrant Smuggling (2021–2025). The renewed Action Plan was adopted by the European Commission in September 2021 as part of the New Pact on Migration and Asylum. In respect to the anti-trafficking governance, the main policy initiatives and the related progress reports were deemed relevant: the EU Strategy towards the Eradication of Trafficking in Human Beings (2012–2016); 2017 Reporting on the follow-up to the EU Strategy towards the Eradication of trafficking in human beings and identifying further concrete actions; EU Strategy on Combatting Trafficking in Human Beings (2021- 2025); Fourth Report on the progress made in the fight against trafficking in human beings.

Findings

In the following section, the results of the analysis of the seven policy documents are presented. The paragraph first considers the anti-smuggling governance framework and how each of the three archframes (two for the diagnosis, one for the prognosis) present themselves within. A symmetrical structure is followed for the paragraph focusing on the anti-trafficking governance. Finally, a discussion of the results in light of the literature review and as an answer to the research question guiding the monograph.

3.1 Smuggling

Feminized vulnerability

The explicit mention of the vulnerability of women is not particularly present in the anti-smuggling documentation, much less than it is in the anti-trafficking framework. The arch-frame has only been identified six times. The 2015-2020 EU Action Plan stated that "the EU should step up efforts to provide smuggled migrants, in particular vulnerable groups such as children and women, with assistance and protection" (European Commission, 2015, p. 8). However, the 2017 REFIT evaluation assessed that, despite efforts, the EU smuggling governance's "lack of gender-specific policy placed women at greater risk" (European Commission, 2017b, p. 51). The 2021-2025 EU Action Plan reiterated that the need to "provide protection and assistance to smuggled vulnerable migrants is key, with a particular attention to children and women" (European Commission, 2021b, p. 19), in light of various situations of vulnerability.

Another common frame appears, that of 'womenandchildren'. In four out of the six codes of feminized vulnerability, the word 'women' is accompanied by the term 'children' when describing who is vulnerable to smuggling. It clearly emerges from the analysis of the arch-frame that women are almost always grouped together with children in one simplified vulnerable group, with little attention paid to the different needs and experiences of the two. Instead, the characteristic that distinguishes them is their *a priori* vulnerability. No explanation or data is given to justify the overemphasis on women and children.

The frames of 'unaware and disinformed victim' and of 'deserving migrant' intertwine to create the idea of a vulnerable figure that has become victim to smuggling because of lack of information or even because "smugglers recruit potential migrants through misinformation campaigns concerning routes, risks and conditions in destination countries" (European Commission, 2021b, p. 5). Smuggled migrants, although entering the EU illegally, may be considered deserving of protection and worthy of integration in view of their vulnerability: "Migrants in an irregular situation are more vulnerable to labor and other forms of exploitation" (European Commission, 2017b, p. 7). In other cases, deservingness translates to the legal right to entry. This is because there is "emerging evidence that smugglers are facilitating the unauthorized movements of beneficiaries of international protection" (European Commission, 2021b, p. 6), who are deemed to deserve to find legal pathways into the EU.

Furthermore, the frames of 'exploitation' and 'abuse' sustain the arch-frame of feminized vulnerability with explicit references to women in two cases within the 2021-2025 EU Action Plan. It states that "children and women may be exposed to violence, exploitation, abuse and trafficking" (European Commission, 2021b, p. 14) and that smugglers "trap them [women] in a web of exploitation and abuse" (European Commission, 2021b, p. 5). In general, the vulnerability of smuggled migrants to abuse and exploitation is a central theme in the documents: "Migrants – particularly those in vulnerable situations such as children and unaccompanied minors – are exposed to violence, extortion, exploitation, rape, abuse, theft, kidnapping and even homicide" (European Commission, 2021b, p. 4). In conclusion, the theme of feminized vulnerability is sustained by the discourse on victimhood and deservingness, with a few frames explicitly mentioning how these are women-specific characteristics.

Masculinized threat

The arch-frame of masculinized threat is not directly present at any point in the selected anti-smuggling documents. In fact, the word 'men' is mentioned only once in the description of the demographics of the migratory flows (European Commission, 2017b, p. 72). However, all other frames extracted from previous literature because of their contribution to the construction of ideas of masculinized threat are prominently featured across the texts. The most common are the ones developed along the socio-economic (32%) and securitarian axes (32%). The 'undeserving migrant' and 'exclusionary effect of vulnerability' frames constitute, respectively, 18% and 10% of the identified codes (see Appendix B). The specific reference to women and children as the only description of vulnerable groups to be protected is prevalent in the documents. The general terminology 'vulnerable migrant' and "other categories of vulnerable persons" (European Commission, 2017b, p. 36) is not sufficient to foster an inclusive understanding of vulnerability. While the particular attention to women and children is based on the empirical reality of situations that are indeed more likely to be dangerous for these groups, the lack of recognition that these are not the only categories who can be rendered vulnerable during the smuggling process impacts men in hidden and exclusionary ways.

The pressure subframe is the least employed, as it constitutes only 8% of codified cases. The documents refer both to the burden on the migration management infrastructures and to the cultural threat posed by the alien nature of smuggled migrants. Firstly, the renewed EU Action Plan describes how increasing numbers of migrants led to a remarkably coordinated response: "The hotspot approach proved essential in the fight against migrant-smuggling with EU agencies – EASO, Frontex, Europol and Eurojust – working closely together with member states facing migratory pressures at the EU's external borders" (European Commission, 2021b, p. 8). Secondly, the alien nature of the migrant wave was expressed by typecasting migrants as racialized men. The REFIT evaluation reported that men comprised the large majority "57%, of the migratory flow", coming primarily from Syria, Afghanistan, and Iraq (European Commission, 2017b, p. 72).

Regarding the socio-economic axis, both subframes of migrants depicted as homines oeconomici and of smuggling as "highly profitable business" (European Commission, 2015, p. 2) were detected. In the renewed EU Action

Plan, it is clearly recognized that migrants are motivated to emigrate in order to pursue better employment opportunities than in their country of origin: "The possibility for irregular migrants to find a job in the informal economy is one of the key drivers of irregular migration" (European Commission, 2021b, p. 3). These opportunities are often in the informal market and, thus, constitute a threat to the EU's market and to migrants' own workers' rights: "Weakening economic conditions in the EU may increase the demand for cheap labor on the black market, which is more likely to attract irregular migrants and lead to labor exploitation, including forced labor" (European Commission, 2021b, p. 4).

Furthermore, the framing of smugglers as participants in a lucrative criminal business model dominates the policy documents of the anti-smuggling regime. Smugglers "generate substantial profits from migrant-smuggling" (European Commission, 2017b, pp. 7-6), "ranging between EUR 4.7 – 6 billion worldwide annually" (European Commission, 2021b, p. 4). It is not only the high price of the trip that is described as both criminal and immoral but also the methods employed by smugglers to gain money. The prevalent description is that of criminals who would do anything to profit off migrants, risking their lives for profit. For example, the EU Action Plan describes that "to maximize their profits, smugglers often squeeze hundreds of migrants onto unseaworthy boats – including small inflatable boats or end-of-life cargo ships - or into trucks" (European Commission, 2015, p. 2).

On the securitarian axis, the documents portray smugglers as hypermasculinized, criminal, and violent figures. Unexpectedly, smuggled migrants are generally not considered a danger to the EU's security and safety, with the exception of "security concerns linked to migrant-smuggling, [such as] crime, terrorism and violent extremism" (European Commission, 2021b, p. 14). On the other hand, smugglers are described as "ruthless criminal networks [that] organize the journeys of large numbers of migrants desperate to reach the EU (European Commission, 2015, p. 1) and who "treat migrants as goods" (European Commission, 2021b, p. 2). The immoral and threatening nature of smugglers is epitomized by the risk they put migrants in and the deaths they cause.

Finally, the frame of the undeserving migrant refers to those who "abuse benefits systems in the EU" (European Commission, 2015, p. 2). The idea of migrants who have no right to stay in the EU after being smuggled into the territory recurs throughout anti-smuggling governance and legitimizes the priority action of "enhancing the effectiveness of return as a deterrent to smuggling" (European Commission, 2015). The measures proposed in the Action Plan and employed under the anti-smuggling framework are grounded on this idea of the bad migrant: "Efforts to crack down on migrant-smuggling must be matched with strong action to return the migrants that have no right to stay in the EU to their home countries" (European Commission, 2015, p. 3).

Prognosis

It is possible to identify a dual framing of the issue of smuggling in the 2015-2020 EU Action Plan against Migrant Smuggling. The dual securitarian-humanitarian object is stated in the very first line of the document: "the fight against migrant-smuggling [was identified] as a priority to prevent the exploitation of migrants by criminal networks and to reduce incentives to irregular migration" (European Commission, 2015, p. 1). On the one hand, the purpose of the Action Plan seems to be the protection of vulnerable migrants. Smugglers are described as "ruthless[ly]" exploiting "desperate migrants" (European Commission, 2015, p. 1), with the EU self-appointing itself as their savior. The plan crudely frames the referent object as the "scores of migrants [who] drown at sea, suffocate in containers or perish in deserts" (European Commission, 2015, p. 2). On the other hand, the link between smuggling and irregular migration also serves as legitimation of the fight against smuggling through the employment of a series of securitized tools. The solutions provided are "enhanced police and judicial response" (European Commission, 2015, p. 2), "improved gathering and information sharing" (p. 4), and "enhanced prevention of smuggling" (p. 6). These actions "should be seen in connection with ongoing work to establish a Common Security and Defense Policy (CSDP) operation to systematically identify, capture and dispose of vessels used by smugglers" (p. 3).

The securitization approach has been operationalized in EU-led military operations. In the 2017 REFIT evaluation, the employment of extraordinary measures since the publication of the first Action Plan is clearly laid out: "Actions set out in the Action Plan are to be seen in complementarity with the ongoing CSDP Operation EUNAVFOR Sophia" (European Commission, 2017b, p. 4). The evaluation attempts to reframe the need to resort to military means by specifying the referent object as the vulnerable migrants that the military operations save: "Operation Sophia involved in SAR interventions in the Mediterranean Sea allowed to save over 228.651 lives in 2016 alone" (European Commission, 2017b, p. 73). Migrants, however, are just one of the referent objects identified in the document. "There is a need to protect the member states' territorial integrity, social cohesion and welfare through well-managed migration flow" (p. 7). Through the expression of such a need, a second referent object is framed: the EU and its security, society, and market.

The dual framing of the referent object can similarly be traced in the renewed 2021-2025 EU Action Plan against Migrant Smuggling. The document represents the EU as threatened by irregular migration and smuggling on the securitarian axis. It is the security of the Union that is jeopardized by the arrival of smuggled migrants and by smugglers. "Organized crime structures capable of carrying out sophisticated operations that cover the full range of migrant-smuggling services constitute a high risk to Europe's security" (European Commission, 2021b, p. 5). Irregular immigration also assumed a new dimension as an existential threat to the EU after episodes of weaponization of migration by state actors "intended to destabilize the European Union and its member states" (European Commission, 2021b, p. 6). In December 2021, the Belarussian regime launched a 'hybrid attack' against the EU to retaliate for the sanctions imposed following the 2020 elections. Migrants were promised easy access to the EU and were gathered at the Baltic border in order to raise pressure on member states.

3.2 Trafficking

Feminized vulnerability

The theme of feminized vulnerability is significantly more present in the documents regulating the anti-trafficking regime rather than in those defining anti-smuggling governance. With 'women' explicitly mentioned 54 times in the four trafficking policy documents over the six times in the smuggling policy documents and with the word 'victim' overwhelmingly characterizing anti-trafficking governance, the correlation between the two terms is evident. The discourse on victimhood is indeed central to trafficking policies, where the protection of victims, in one form or the other, as "protecting, supporting, and empowering victims" (European Commission, 2021a) has been a key pillar of the framework. Turning to Critical Frame Analysis, the arch-frame of feminized vulnerability has been defined in the codebook as the explicit reference to the vulnerability of women, and it appears 37 times throughout the anti-trafficking policy framework.

The arch-frame of feminized vulnerability is substantially present throughout the anti-trafficking policy documentation. However, the strength of the methodology of Critical Frame Analysis, as has been previously noted, lies in its ability to uncover the unstated prejudices that influence the construction of the arch-frame. A variety of regular frames contribute to the construction of vulnerability without necessarily mentioning gender but relying on stereotypically feminine characteristics. Some of the frames are expressed through explicit mentions of women or 'gender' – in its narrow conceptualization where it is equated to women –while others' only connection to women derives from their past use as representations of stereotypically feminine behaviors or traits. The following sections analyze how the frames in the codebook contribute to framing certain individuals as vulnerable referent objects. All five frames have been utilized to some degree in the construction of vulnerability to trafficking. The MAXQDA statistics reveal that the one most commonly employed was that of 'womenandchildren' (28.6%), followed by 'unaware and disinformed victims' and 'sexual exploitation' (20%), 'deserving migrant' (15.7%), and finally 'abuse and gender-based violence' (8.6%) (see Appendix B).

Since trafficking in children is widespread – in 2021, "nearly a quarter of all victims of trafficking were children" (European Commission, 2021a, p. 12), the policies' focus on child trafficking is not surprising. What is interesting about the research is to note how mentions of children are often accompanied by mentions of women. The actual phrase "women and children" appears seven times throughout the selected documents, but other uses of the frame were identified, for example, with the remarks of "gender-specific and child-sensitive aspects" (European Commission, 2021, p. 5). The link between women and children has been sustained by three motivations. Firstly, similarly to women, "most of the child victims are trafficked for sexual exploitation" (European Commission, 2021, p. 12). Secondly, "the majority of child victims are female (75%)" (European Commission, 2022, p. 7). Thirdly, traffickers employ similar methods to entrap 'young women' and children, such as "the use of the 'lover boy' method by traffickers to lure children and young adult women into sexual exploitation" (European Commission, 2022, p. 7).

In most other cases, women and children are grouped into the same 'especially vulnerable' category without considering the different backstories, characteristics, and sensitivities of the two.

The frame of the 'unaware and misinformed victims' emerges in the activation of awareness campaigns proposed by the Commission to address trafficking. In the 2012-2016 EU Strategy, 'EU-wide Awareness Raising Activities' was a priority action that led to the implementation of "numerous awareness-raising campaigns, locally, nationally, internationally and in third countries" (European Commission, 2012, p. 12). All the selected documents envisaged such measures to raise awareness among different audiences, always including the victims. Misinformation lies at the heart of recruitment of potential victims, who are "recruited in the country of origin, sometimes with the promise of a respectable job in the EU" (European Commission, 2022, p. 8). If that does not work, a mix of "violence, threats, manipulation and deception are used to recruit and exploit victims" (European Commission, 2021, p. 10). The blurred line between voluntary and trafficked migrants was also described as a byproduct of unawareness: "traffickers lure victims to enter voluntary business agreements. Persons in this type of arrangement do not necessarily perceive themselves as victims" (European Commission, 2022, p. 5).

'Deserving migrants' receive access to benefits, such as legal status or protection, in view of their vulnerability. As trafficked persons are recognized as victims, they are awarded additional advantages compared to smuggled migrants. In the documents, they are presented as already possessing them or as deserving of gaining them. For example, trafficked persons might already have legal status: "There are numerous cases of trafficking of migrants who had arrived in the EU through legal routes and were later exploited (European Commission, 2022). However, migrants who were victims of trafficking and have reached the EU illegally "should receive appropriate protection and assistance" (European Commission, 2012, p. 6), according to the Anti-Trafficking Directive. This includes "immediate assistance, support and protection as well as a re-integration perspective for a better life for them" (European Commission, 2021, p. 2). The 2021-2025 EU Strategy discourages the return of victims who are irregular migrants because they "can become accessible to traffickers and be exposed to risks of being re-trafficked" (European Commission, 2021, p. 15).

Masculinized threat

The arch-frame of masculinized threat, described in the codebook as the explicit reference to the dangerousness of men, is rarely present. Among the selected anti-trafficking documents, the reference to men as threats occur once in the 2021-2015 EU strategy reporting the empirical reality that "nearly three-quarters of perpetrators are men" (European Commission, 2021a, p. 2). On the contrary, when the word 'men' is employed in nine cases out of ten, it is to make explicit the role of men as victims of trafficking. The recognition of men as vulnerable is an unexpected finding that has been integrated as its own arch-frame into the codebook and is further analyzed in the section 'findings countering the hypotheses'. Nevertheless, through Critical Frame Analysis, it is possible to uncover the frames that sustain masculinized threat without the necessary mention of 'men'. The following paragraphs analyze how the frames in the codebook contribute to framing certain individuals as dangerous existential threats on the basis of previously identified masculinized securitarian, socio-economic, and identitarian axes of threat, in addition to the other masculinized traits of 'undeserving migrant' and non-vulnerable men.

The trope of the 'undeserving migrant' does not recur in the anti-trafficking documents, while it is much more common in the anti-smuggling governance. This is because, in anti-trafficking policies, migrants are primarily considered victims who "should not be penalized for crimes they were compelled to commit during their exploitation" (European Commission, 2021a, p. 15). This also includes the crime of irregular migration and entry into the EU, which is overshadowed by the critical role of victims in identifying and prosecuting perpetrators: "Victims should not have to fear retaliation and secondary victimization during criminal proceedings" (European Commission, 2021, p. 13). Importantly, the deservingness discourse is explicitly gendered in the 2021-2025 EU Strategy, where "a strong gender dimension in supporting and protecting victims, the non-punishment of victims for crimes they were compelled to commit, and in relation to residence permit for victims of trafficking" (European Commission, 2021, p. 16) is prioritized. Consequently, the latter is considered an expression of women being regarded as 'good' migrants, in general, and men being excluded from such categorization.

The exclusion of men from the trope of the 'deserving migrant' is sustained by the so-called "hidden exclusionary effect" (Hruschka & Leboeuf, 2019).

This mechanism is clear in the case of vulnerability. Every time women (and children) are categorized as vulnerable, men are excluded from such categorization. It leads to men's decreased access to benefits, resources, and advantages. This is implicitly justified by the idea that they do not deserve access to it because they are not vulnerable. This is sustained in the documents by the neglect to focus on men in empirical data. For example, while the 2017 Reporting specifies that sexual exploitation is comprised of women, it does not mention that labor exploitation is equally largely comprised of men (European Commission, 2017a, p. 8).

The 'undeservingness' of male migrants is motivated on the basis of the assumptions developed along Ceyhan and Tsoukala (2002)'s axes. In anti-trafficking documents, the identitarian frame has not been identified: the cultural threat from the increased number of third-country nationals in the EU is not considered as such within anti-trafficking governance, to the point that different policies are instead aimed at their protection. For example, under the 2004 Residence Permit Directive, "third-country nationals are granted a reflection period allowing them to recover and escape the influence of the perpetrators" (European Commission, 2021a, p. 16), during which they receive accommodation and protection from deportation. On the contrary, both the securitarian and socio-economic frames have been identified in the selected documents on trafficking. The securitarian frame is the one that has most largely been utilized, comprising 65.8% of the codes under the arch-frame of masculinized threat, while the socio-economic frame is less conspicuous, encompassing 21.1% of the codes under the arch-frame (see Appendix B).

Within the socio-economic frame, the subframe of the 'financial gains' of traffickers dominates over that of the trafficked as an immoral '*homo oeconomicus*'. The former appears eight times throughout the selected documents, while the latter is only two. Documents note that "irregular migration created profit opportunities for trafficking networks" (European Commission, 2022, p. 8), which is a "lucrative form of crime generating profits of dozens of billions of euro for the perpetrators each year" (European Commission, 2012, p. 2). Solutions include actions to "deprive traffickers of their financial gain and thus ensuring that the crime does not pay" (European Commission, 2021a, p. 6). Moreover, the idea of '*homo oeconomicus*' is rather inserted in a discourse that does not label those who were trafficked for labor exploitation as threats but as victims. Victims of traffic were also targeted by "awareness-raising campaigns on labor rights and safe work opportunities" (European Commission, 2022, p. 12).

Finally, the prominence of the securitarian frame promotes the securitization of the figure of traffickers on the basis of three subframes: 'criminal behavior', 'hypermasculinization', and 'violence'. The subframe depicting either traffickers or migrants as sexual predators was not found in the documents, despite the expectations set by previous literature. Firstly, the criminal nature of trafficking is unequivocally remarked. Trafficking is described as "a violent crime committed by organized crime networks" (European Commission, 2021a, p. 2), "a complex criminal phenomenon" (European Commission, 2021, p. 3), and "a highly profitable form of serious and organized crime" (European Commission, 2017a, p. 2). Secondly, traffickers are hyper-masculinized through the employment of harsh language, such as that they "prey on social inequalities" (European Commission, 2021, p. 2) and cause "tremendous suffering to victims" (p. 20). Thirdly, a related 'violence' subframe underscores the representation of traffickers. "Lover boys resort more quickly and frequently to threatening their victims, using blackmail and violence" (European Commission, 2022, p. 8) and, in general, "violence, threats, manipulation and deception are used to recruit and exploit victims" (European Commission, 2021, p. 10).

Findings countering the hypotheses

The existence of the frame 'recognition of men as vulnerable' redresses the expectations of the research regarding who is represented as vulnerable and who is threatening. The 2012-2016 EU Strategy recognizes that vulnerability is a condition in which anyone, regardless of gender, can find themselves in: "Trafficking in human beings [...] targets women and men, girls, and boys in vulnerable positions" (European Commission, 2012, p. 2). However, such a framing rarely appears in later documents, which rather focus on the fact that there exists gender-specific and age-specific vulnerabilities. While this is an undeniable fact, the sole focus on gender and age as special conditions for receiving protection results in the "hidden exclusionary effect" (Hruschka & Leboeuf, 2019) of other vulnerable people. The "incorporation of a gender perspective" (European Commission, 2012, p. 12) refers to the special attention to be dedicated to women and, consequently, moved away from men.

In other contexts, gender sensitivity and gender are used according to the correct feminist conceptualization, comprising both women and men, femininity, and masculinity. When the EU Strategy towards the Eradication of Trafficking in Human Beings (2012–2016) refers to the "gender dimension of human trafficking", it acknowledges the "gender specificities of the way men and women are recruited and exploited, the gender consequences of the various forms of trafficking and potential differences in the vulnerability of men and women to victimization and its impact on them" (European Commission, 2012, p. 13). The 2012-2016 EU Strategy embodies the empirical data on the gendered distribution in various forms of exploitation and explicitly recognizes that "vulnerability to trafficking and to different forms of exploitation is shaped by gender" (European Commission, 2012, p. 13). In fact, women and girls tend to be trafficked for purposes of sexual exploitation or labor exploitation in the domestic and care sectors, while men and boys tend to be trafficked for purposes of forced labor in a variety of fields, such as agriculture, construction, mining, forestry, and fishing. Because of the different types of exploitation they are subjected to, the "short and long-term consequences on trafficked women and men might differ" (European Commission, 2012, p. 13).

While it is impressive that an early document had already overcome what the literature had identified as a major obstacle to a comprehensive and holistic representation of migrants' and trafficked persons' victimhood – as it was assumed that it would be essentialized to notions of feminized vulnerability –, it should be noted that the frame is restricted to Action 2 ("Developing knowledge relating to the gender dimension of trafficking and vulnerable groups") under the priority area of increasing knowledge and effective response to emerging concerns. While the idea that men can also be vulnerable was at least expressed in the document, it was in relation to knowledge-development tasks assigned to the Commission for the future. Looking at successive documents, the focus moves back to women-specific vulnerabilities, and men are rarely mentioned as vulnerable. In conclusion, throughout the rest of the document and even in all other documents, the frame is rarely utilized.

A few exceptions can be found in two of the selected documents published after 2012. In the 2017 Reporting, in order to ensure that victims are protected and their rights respected – one of the priorities of the Strategy –the

Commission encourages member states to "tak[e] account of the specific needs of each gender" (European Commission, 2017a, p. 6) when designing comprehensive protection systems and managing the integration of victims into their societies. The importance of the mention of a gender-sensitive approach lies in the fact, firstly, that men are recognized among the victims of trafficking and, secondly, that their needs differ from those of women. Furthermore, in the 2021-2025 EU Strategy the only reference to men as victims is when appropriate accommodation for victims is discussed: "safe shelters are needed for children, women and men" (European Commission, 2021a, p. 16). At the same time, the emphasis on the value of same-sex shelters providing trauma-focused support evokes the picture of women's shelters for domestic violence.

Prognosis

The earliest policy document analyzed, the EU Strategy Towards the Eradication of Trafficking in Human Beings for the period 2012–2016, published in 2012, set up a multi-objective framework for the management of trafficking. It identified five priorities: identifying, protecting and assisting victims of trafficking; stepping up the prevention of trafficking in human beings; increased prosecution of traffickers; enhanced coordination and cooperation among key actors and policy coherence; increased knowledge of and effective response to emerging concerns related to all forms of trafficking in human beings (European Commission, 2012, p. 5), It is possible to note that the first, fourth and fifth priorities are centered around the idea of protecting victims of trafficking. The securitization of policies, thus, is justified by the idea that migrants who have been trafficked are the referent objects to be protected.

At the same time, prosecution of traffickers, who were recognized as the major cause of the threat, was also central to the strategy. The dual approach against trafficking was made more explicit in successive documents. The 2017 Reporting clearly states that "the EU remains committed to preventing and combating trafficking in human beings and to protecting victims' rights" (European Commission, 2017a, p. 2). The two objectives can be interrelated as "disrupting the business model that trafficking in human beings depends on improv[es] victims' access to rights" (European Commission, 2017, p. 3). In the document it is clear that the ultimate referent objects are trafficked victims, "behind each of whom lies devastating experiences and suffering" (European Commission, 2017a, p. 2). The strong language describing why victims need protection justifies the need to adopt "stronger action", particularly in view of co-challenging events, such as "the global financial crisis, the migration crisis and the security threats posed by organized crime groups [that] further exacerbate vulnerabilities" (European Commission, 2017, p. 3). Extraordinary measures were to be activated, including "action taken under the mandates of the Common Security and Defense Policy missions and operations including for counter-terrorism activity" (European Commission, 2017, p. 8).

The securitization of trafficking only gained favor in 2015. The 2021-2025 EU Strategy highlights that "combating trafficking in human beings has long been a priority for the European Union" (European Commission, 2021a, p. 3) and encourages to continue to "reinforce the Union's response [as] the threat of being trafficked remains high for any vulnerable person" (European Commission, 2021, p. 20). The renewed EU Strategy maintains the focus on trafficked victims as the referent object, emphasizing how "trafficking destroys individuals' lives by depriving people of their dignity, freedom and fundamental rights" (European Commission, 2021, p. 2) and "causes great suffering and long-lasting harm to the victims" (European Commission, 2021, p. 13). However, it also identifies a different referent object. The renewed EU Strategy is the sole document among those selected where the securitization of trafficking is presented as a solution with the purpose of protecting not only migrants but also the EU itself: "The fight against trafficking is essential for ensuring European security, protecting vulnerable people and the economy, and for the safeguarding of the rule of law and fundamental rights" (European Commission, 2021, p. 21).

The goal of "preventing infiltration into the legal economy and society" of the EU (European Commission, 2021, p. 10) was advanced through the recourse to extraordinary measures. Especially regarding external action, securitized and militarized responses were prioritized. The renewed EU Strategy recognized that "the EU's approach to external security within the framework of the Common Foreign and Security and the Common Security and Defense Policy is essential" (European Commission, 2021, p. 19). CSDP civilian and military missions led "efforts to disrupt organized criminal networks involved in smuggling of migrants and trafficking in human beings" (European Commission, 2021, p. 19). Furthermore, the Global Strategy for the EU Foreign and Security Policy "facilitated and supported closer coop-eration with non-EU countries" (European Commission, 2021, p. 18). The activation of foreign policy instruments, including military operations, in order to manage trafficking to this extent is novel. Arguably, the framing of the EU as the referent object reinforced the securitization of the issue and allowed deeper mobilization of extraordinary resources.

3.3 Discussion

The analysis provided an answer to the specific research question: *How does gender influence the securitization of smuggling and trafficking in the European Union (EU)?* It demonstrated that the gendered constructions of 'feminine' vulnerability and 'masculine' threat are among the security frames underpin-ning the securitization of the EU's smuggling and trafficking policies. While it is true that the explicit connection between women and vulnerability as well as men and dangerousness has been identified, its presence in the selected documents was not always considerable. The employment of Critical Frame Analysis, however, allows to detect and expose the underlying frames and the unstated prejudices that influence the construction of the arch-frames of feminized vulnerability and masculinized threat. A variety of regular frames contribute to the construction of vulnerability without necessarily mentioning gender but relying on stereotypically feminine characteristics, and, vice versa, support the construction of threat on the basis of archetypal masculine traits. These underscore ideas of vulnerability and threat that are not necessarily specific to women or men but that are either feminized or masculinized.

In anti-smuggling governance, the representation of smuggled migrants as threats or referent objects is based on the gender binary while smugglers are undoubtedly framed as threatening. A dual representation of smuggled migrants as both threats and referent objects coexists within anti-smuggling documents. On the one hand, feminized characteristics, in addition to explicit mentions of women as vulnerable, contribute to framing smuggled migrants as referent objects to be protected and aided. Their vulnerability to abuse and exploitation is a recurring theme, especially concerning women, and it is seen as the result of strategic use of misinformation on the part of smugglers, who lie to migrants about the conditions of the journey or the employment opportunities in host countries in order to convince them to undertake the journey. The fibbed, exploited, and abused migrant is evidently vulnerable and is deemed deserving of receiving protection by the EU, regardless of the fact that they entered Schengen irregularly.

On the other hand, smuggled migrants are seen as threats. According to Ceyhan and Tsoukala (2002), they threaten different referent objects within the EU. The analysis reveals that anti-smuggling documents focus in particular on the threat their increasing numbers pose to the identity and the socio-economic status of EU citizens. A gendered dimension is complicit in such a framing. Men, as the largest portion of migratory groups, are considered responsible for the pressure they apply on migration management infrastructures and their racialized origins makes them a threat to cultural homogeneity and European identity and customs. Furthermore, they are motivated to immigrate by the pursuit of new and better employment opportunities, which affects local European workers in two ways. Firstly, it creates more competition in environments with already scarce demand. Secondly, it affects the welfare resources available for the local population, that are consumed by migrants. Thus, they are framed as 'bad' and undeserving of being granted access to the EU and all of the related benefits.

Nevertheless, the biggest villains in the document are the smugglers, who are hypermasculinized as money-hungry, avid criminals who are willing to risk the lives of migrants – who, in this case, return to be referent objects – in order to maximize their profits. They are described as violent, ruthless, and deceptive. Smugglers are rarely conceptualized as individuals and personified, rather they are described as highly sophisticated criminal networks with ties to armed groups and local militias. This representation is simplistic and does not reflect the reality of the complex phenomenon that smuggling is. Carrera et al. (2019) found that the "relationships between migrants and their smugglers have many faces, and rarely conform to the mainstream notion of helpless migrant and ruthless smuggler" (p. 17). In fact, the relationship between migrants and smugglers is complex and goes beyond simple exploitation. The recounts of the interaction with smugglers collected by Freedman (2016b) reveal that for some migrants the role of smugglers had become normalized and was perceived as an ordinary part of the journey. Others, primarily women, revealed that they had instead been traumatized by the experience.

In anti-trafficking governance's policy documents, trafficked migrants, either male or female, are overwhelmingly considered to be victims, although with gendered differences regarding incidence and purposes. On the other hand, traffickers are framed as threats to both the trafficked and the EU. Trafficking is clearly demonstrated to be a gendered phenomenon requiring gender-sensitive measures. The predominance of the archframe of feminized vulnerability, where women are explicitly categorized as vulnerable, is based on the empirical data which confirms that women comprise most of the trafficked persons. While particular attention is paid to women (and children), the anti-trafficking framework acknowledges that the vulnerability of victims does not only depend on the gender of the trafficked person, but on a series of intersectional factors, including social class and level of education. The 2012-2016 EU Strategy recognizes that vulnerability is a condition to which anyone, regardless of gender, can be subjected once they are trafficked. Anti-trafficking documents continued to occasionally recognize the vulnerability of men, alongside that of women and children, and to adopt truly gender-specific measures that considered the different needs of men and women as a result of the different types of trafficking of which they were victim, respectively labor and sexual exploitation.

Additionally, feminized traits also contributed to the victim-centered representation of trafficked persons. Men, women, and children are often recruited by traffickers under the false guise of smuggling them out of the countries. Traffickers use misinformation to convince unaware migrants to enter situations of vulnerability, where they can more easily be exploited. Alternatively, individuals are coerced through violence, threats, and manipulation into a cycle of exploitation and trafficking that they are not free to leave. The lack of consent and the element of coercion distinguish victims of trafficking from smuggled migrants. The former are then categorized as deserving migrants in a host country in light of their undeniable vulnerability. As trafficked persons are recognized as victims, they are granted additional benefits and advantages compared to smuggled migrants. For example, they are allotted a reflection period during which they cannot be deported to their country of origin or a transit country. The anti-trafficking regime prioritizes protecting and assisting victims of trafficking, that are framed as the principal referent object of the trafficking threat.

On the contrary, the existential threat from which victims need to be protected are traffickers. The gendered nature of the phenomenon is also reflected in the construction of the threat. With the majority of traffickers empirically demonstrated to be men, the threat is immediately masculinized. In general, traffickers are framed as dangerous existential threats on the basis of previously identified masculinized securitarian and socio-economic axes of threat. They are defined as violent criminals partaking in a highly profitable criminal phenomenon. Their use of coercion and other violent methods, which is among the defining characteristics of trafficking, relates to the hypermasculine stereotype of men as inherently violent. Hypermasculinization also applies to additional specific methods of recruitment of victims, such as the 'lover boy method', identified in the 2021-2015 EU Strategy, centered around the figure of a male trafficker seducing his victims in order to put them in a situation of vulnerability and exploit them.

The analysis confirmed some of the expectations put forward in the early phases of the monograph, but it also produced unexpected results regarding who is considered vulnerable in the anti-trafficking regime. Given that the frames of feminized vulnerability are recurrent in the selected policy documents, it is a possibility that, while men are indeed considered vulnerable, it is because they have been feminized. The process of femininization consists in the transfer of typically feminine characteristics, such as vulnerability, to any subject, including male ones. Sachseder et al. (2022) found that Frontex had alternately masculinized and feminized migrants in its risk analysis any time it deemed fit, making women dangerous and racialized men vulnerable. A similar process may have occurred within anti-trafficking governance, whereby the recognition of men as vulnerable relies on feminized traits of vulnerability, deserving migrants, and unaware victims.

The analysis demonstrated that the securitization of smuggling and trafficking occurred on the basis of a gendered process. By retracing this process following the steps first identified by Buzan et al. (1998), it is noticeable that, while EU anti-smuggling and anti-trafficking governance developed in the early 2000s alongside the creation of international regimes, the challenging event that accelerated the securitization of the policies was the 2015 migration crisis. The enhanced pressure on the EU's border management system, the tragically high number of deaths at sea of smuggled migrants, and the protraction of the trafficking phenomenon despite the development of a legal framework and of operationalized strategies focused the attention of European policy-makers, media, and public on combating smuggling and trafficking. Different securitizing moves were attempted in order to frame the issue as a threat and justify the mobilization of extraordinary resources, as illustrated by Hintjens (2019). This paper concentrates on the EU and its policy-makers as the securitizing actor. However, since the media is another relevant actor, as highlighted by previous studies (de Norohna, 2015; Gray & Franck, 2019; Pruitt et al., 2018; Scheibelhofer, 2017; Wyss, 2022), further research may analyze the securitizing moves by newspapers and journalists regarding smuggling and trafficking.

The securitizing moves have been successful in framing smuggling and trafficking as threats. The discourse in the documents is underlined by aggressive and defensive language describing the "fight against" smuggling and trafficking, with the objective to "combat", "crack down", and "tackle" the phenomena (European Commission, 2012, 2015, 2017a, 2017b, 2021a, 2021b, 2022). Such a framing has been accepted by the audience and has become the centerpiece of anti-smuggling and anti-trafficking policies. The audience's acceptance legitimized the EU as a provider of security to resort to extraordinary and exceptional measures. The most evident expression of this trend is that anti-smuggling and anti-trafficking actions are now included under Common Security and Defense Policy operations. EU-led military actions include the naval force operations IRINI and ATALANTA aimed at disrupting the business model of migrant-smuggling and trafficking in human beings. The mobilization of military resources for the fight against smuggling and trafficking is epitomized by Operation Sophia, whose "prominent military nature" (Carrera et al., 2019) is aimed at the "ultimate goal" of the war on smugglers (Moreno-Lax, 2018).

The success of the securitizing moves lies in the framing of the referent object to be protected from the threat. Anti-smuggling and anti-trafficking governance identify two concurrent referent objects, advancing a dual securitarian-humanitarian framing of the issue. On the one hand, the EU is represented as a referent object to be protected from smuggled migrants, but especially from traffickers and smugglers. This framing is characterized by ideas of masculinized threat, whereby hypermasculinized, violent, and criminal traffickers and smugglers contribute to endangering the security of the EU by facilitating irregular immigration. Smuggled migrants, but not trafficked victims, are also occasionally represented as a threat to Europe's security and labor market on the basis of masculinized characteristics. On the other hand, migrants themselves are presented as the referent object. While Hintjens (2019) found that it was counterproductive to frame refugees as at risk after decade-long campaigns depicting them as threats, the analysis demonstrated that the employment of the frame of feminized vulnerability was actually successful in advancing such a framing, especially in regard to trafficked victims. The humanitarian frame of the feminized vulnerable trafficked and smuggled migrant was key in justifying the securitization of the issues and the employment of military means to address them.

Conclusion

The analysis conducted in the monograph provides insights into the research question seeking to understand the influence of gender on the securitization of migration at the EU level. As a case study, the securitization of the EU's smuggling and trafficking governance has been qualitatively analyzed in search of gendered framings of the referent objects and the existential threats. The findings confirm that the securitization process is deeply rooted in gendered constructions of vulnerability and threat based on stereotypes of femininity and masculinity. Importantly, these ideas of vulnerability and threat may not be specific to women or men but are instead feminized or masculinized. Thus, it is possible to conclude that the securitization of smuggling and trafficking within the EU is deeply gendered. The 2015 migration crisis served as a pivotal event that accelerated the securitization of these policies, framing these issues as threats and mobilizing extraordinary resources, such as the launch of CSDP operations. The success of these securitizing moves is evident in the acceptance and legitimation of the EU's role as a security provider.

Employing Critical Frame Analysis, the monograph has shown that gender matters for the securitization of smuggling and trafficking. The connection between gender and securitization is evident in the four arch-frames that dominate the selected policy documents: feminized vulnerability, masculinized threat, recognition of men as vulnerable, and securitization. The themes are present at varying degrees throughout the documents, and their interrelation similarly fluctuates. Feminized vulnerability is one of the dominant arch-frames through which securitization of smuggling and trafficking is legitimized. It happens on the basis of a humanitarian framing of the issue: as envisioned by Moreno-Lax (2018), humanitarian notions are used as justifications to advance the securitization of migration. The language of humanitarianism and its victimhood discourse are co-opted to motivate the employment of militarized measures, such as the launch of Common Security and Defense Policy (CSDP) operations, in order to protect the referent object of migrants. The arch-frame is present both in anti-smuggling and anti-trafficking documents, although the victim-centered focus is much more prominent in the latter.

An additional arch-frame emerged from the analysis of anti-trafficking documents. In the anti-trafficking regime, the framing of trafficked migrants overwhelmingly categorizes them as victims, irrespective of gender. Documents repeatedly recognize that men are also vulnerable to exploitation, abuse, and trafficking. In particular, the different gendered purposes for which women and men are trafficked are acknowledged: while women are primarily victims of sexual exploitation, men are, for the most part, subjected to labor exploitation. However, the analysis also reveals that the recognition of men as vulnerable in the anti-trafficking regime relies on typically feminine characteristics, implying that men's vulnerability is understood through the transfer of feminized traits and not as their own distinctive condition. For example, the victim-centered representation of trafficked persons emphasizes feminized traits of vulnerability and deservingness.

The arch-frame of masculinized threat is applied to smugglers and smuggled migrants in the anti-smuggling regime and primarily to traffickers in the anti-trafficking regime. Smuggled migrants are dually represented as referent objects according to their feminine characteristics and as threats according to their masculine traits. The threat posed by the increasing numbers of migrants to the identity and socio-economic status of EU citizens is masculinized. Men, as the predominant portion of migratory groups, are seen as responsible for exerting pressure on migration management infrastructures, and racialized men, in particular, are viewed as threats to cultural homogeneity and European identity. Moreover, traffickers and smugglers are characterized as dangerous existential threats and hypermasculinized as money-hungry, ruthless criminals willing to endanger and exploit the lives of migrants to maximize their profits. This characterization justifies the militarized and aggressive nature of EU operations and policies aiming to "crack down on" and "tackle" the phenomena.

A few notes on the methodology and future research are imperative. Critical Frame Theory is a powerful instrument for the analysis of policy documents. Despite the seemingly neutral and unbiased form of the texts, policies are the results of negotiations and debates, and they reflect the interplay between the dominant political, public, and legal narratives of the time. They reproduce the patriarchal stereotypes that understate public discourse and cognitive thinking of the general public and policy-makers themselves. Critical Frame Analysis subtly recognizes prejudices beyond what is simply stated in a policy. Verloo and Lombardo (2007), who first conceptualized this version of the methodology, asked themselves, "How does a researcher know s/he is answering to what the text says or to what s/he thinks the text is saying?" (p. 40)? They conclude that subjective interpretation can be avoided by contrasting interpretations with the context in which the documents originated. Future research may overcome such a limitation by conducting a triangular analysis of policy documents, media articles, and legislation in order to consider whether and how gendered constructions are present in the larger context.

Furthermore, future research is needed to expand the empirical applications of the framework on migration, gender, and securitization. This monograph adds to the work on policies by Stachowitsch and Sachseder (2019), Sachseder et al. (2022), and Welfens (2020), who have investigated how gendered constructions contribute to the securitization of migration management, respectively, in the risk analysis documents of Frontex and the European Agenda on Migration. However, these studies and the monograph only scratch the surface of the vast migration management architecture that the EU has developed over the years, especially since 2015. Additional studies investigating the gendered assumptions that sustain the securitization of policies at the heart of Fortress Europe are necessary to gain a comprehensive image of the securitization of migration in the EU.

In light of recent international and internal developments, a potentially interesting case study would be the activation of the Temporary Protection Directive (Council of the EU, 2001), triggered for the first time in response to the Russian invasion of Ukraine on 24 February 2022. The case study could be of interest for three reasons. Firstly, Directive 2001/55/EC is part of the asylum system, an area where the communitarization of policies has peaked, and the EU has substantial supranational competencies. Secondly, the Directive has been activated in the highly securitized context of war, although it has seemingly favored a victim-centered approach. Finally, the gender dimension is significant, as 90% of estimated refugees are women and children (UNHCR, 2023). Further research analyzing the role of gender in securitization will positively affect the whole field of security studies, providing a more comprehensive and authentic understanding of reality and security. In fact, "to talk about security without thinking about gender is simply to account for the surface reflections without examining what is happening deep down below the surface" (Booth, 1994).

References

An area of freedom, security and justice: General aspects | Fact Sheets on the European Union. (2022, May 31). European Parliament. https://www.europarl.europa.eu/factsheets/en/sheet/150/an-area-of-freedom-security-and-justice-general-aspects

Andersson, R. (2014). *Illegality, Inc.: Clandestine Migration and the Business of Bordering Europe* (1st ed.). University of California Press. https://www.jstor.org/stable/10.1525/j.ctt6wqc7v

Arrouche, K., Fallone, A., & Vosyliūtė, L. (2021). *Between politics and inconvenient evidence. Assessing the renewed EU Action Plan against smuggling.*

Asderaki, F., & Markozani, E. (2021). The Securitization of Migration and the 2015 Refugee Crisis: From Words to Actions. In A. Tziampiris & F. Asderaki (Eds.), *The New Eastern Mediterranean Transformed: Emerging Issues and New Actors* (pp. 179–198). Springer International Publishing. https://doi.org/10.1007/978-3-030-70554-1_9

Asylum-seekers. (2023). UNHCR. https://www.unhcr.org/asylum-seekers

Balzacq, T. (Ed.). (2010). *Securitization Theory: How Security Problems Emerge and Dissolve*. Routledge. https://doi.org/10.4324/9780203868508

Bello, V. (2022). The spiralling of the securitisation of migration in the EU: From the management of a 'crisis' to a governance of human mobility? *Journal of Ethnic and Migration Studies, 48*(6), 1327–1344. https://doi.org/10.1080/1369183X.2020.1851464

Booth, K. (1994). *Security and Self Reflections of a Fallen Realist*. YCISS. https://yorkspace.library.yorku.ca/xmlui/handle/10315/1414

Buzan, B. (1983). *People, States, and Fear: The National Security Problem in International Relations*. Wheatsheaf Books.

Buzan, B., Buzan, R. P. of I. S. C. for the S. of D. B., Wæver, O., Waever, O., & Wilde, J. de. (1998). *Security: A New Framework for Analysis*. Lynne Rienner Publishers.

Ceccorulli, M. (2019). Back to Schengen: The collective securitisation of the EU free-border area. *West European Politics, 42*(2), 302–322. https://doi.org/10.1080/01402382.2018.1510196

Ceyhan, A., & Tsoukala, A. (2002). The Securitization of Migration in Western Societies: Ambivalent Discourses and Policies. *Alternatives, 27*(1_suppl), 21–39. https://doi.org/10.1177/03043754020270S103

Council of the EU (2001, July 20). *Council Directive 2001/55/EC of 20 July 2001 on minimum standards for giving temporary protection in the event of a mass influx of displaced persons and on measures promoting a balance of efforts between Member States in receiving such persons and bearing the consequences thereof.* http://data.europa.eu/eli/dir/2001/55/oj/eng

Crenshaw, K. (1991). Mapping the Margins: Intersectionality, Identity Politics, and Violence against Women of Color. *Stanford Law Review, 43*(6), 1241–1299. https://doi.org/10.2307/1229039

d'Appollonia, A. C. (2012). The Framing of Immigration as a Security Issue. In *Frontiers of Fear: Immigration and Insecurity in the United States*. Cornell University Press. http://ezproxy.unibo.it/login?url=https://search.ebscohost.com/login.aspx?direct=true&db=nlebk&AN=671378&site=ehost-live&scope=site

Derrida, J. (2000). *Of Hospitality*. Stanford University Press.

Donato, K. M., Gabaccia, D., Holdaway, J., Manalansan, M., & Pessar, P. R. (2006). A Glass Half Full? Gender in Migration Studies. *International Migration Review, 40*(1), 3–26. https://doi.org/10.1111/j.1747-7379.2006.00001.x

Eurobarometer 84. (2015, November). European Commission. https://europa.eu/eurobarometer/surveys/detail/2098

European Commission (2012). *The EU Strategy towards the Eradication of Trafficking in Human Beings 2012–2016*. https://eur-lex.europa.eu/legal-content/EN/TXT/?uri=celex%3A52012DC0286

European Commission (2015). *EU Action Plan against Migrant Smuggling (2015—2020)*. https://eur-lex.europa.eu/legal-content/EN/TXT/?uri=celex%3A52015DC0285

European Commission (2016). *Proposal For A Regulation Of The European Parliament And Of The Council establishing a Union Resettlement Framework and amending Regulation (EU) No 516/2014 of the European Parliament and the Council*. https://eur-lex.europa.eu/legal-content/EN/TXT/PDF/?uri=CELEX:52016PC0468

European Commission (2017a). *Reporting on the follow-up to the EU Strategy towards the Eradication of trafficking in human beings and identifying further concrete actions*. https://eur-lex.europa.eu/legal-content/EN/ALL/?uri=CELEX:52017DC0728

European Commission (2017b). *REFIT Evaluation of the EU legal framework against facilitation of unauthorised entry, transit and residence: The Facilitators Package (Directive 2002/90/EC and Framework Decision 2002/946/JHA)*. https://www.europarl.europa.eu/RegData/docs_autres_institutions/commission_europeenne/swd/2017/0117/COM_SWD(2017)0117_EN.pdf

European Commission (2017c). *Seventh Report on the Progress made in the implementation of the EU-Turkey*. (2017, September 6). EUR-Lex. https://eur-lex.europa.eu/legal-content/EN/TXT/?uri=COM:2017:0470:FIN

European Commission (2021a). *EU Strategy on Combatting Trafficking in Human Beings 2021- 2025*. https://eur-lex.europa.eu/legal-content/EN/TXT/?uri=CELEX:52021DC0171

European Commission (2021b). *A renewed EU Action Plan against Migrant Smuggling (2021-2025)*. https://eur-lex.europa.eu/legal-content/EN/TXT/?uri=CELEX%3A52021DC0591

European Commission (2022). *Report on the progress made in the fight against trafficking in human beings (Fourth Report)*. https://eur-lex.europa.eu/legal-content/EN/TXT/?uri=CELEX%3A52022DC0736

European Parliament & Council of the EU (2011). *Directive 2011/95/EU of the European Parliament and of the Council of 13 December 2011 on standards for the qualification of third-country nationals or stateless persons as beneficiaries of international protection, for a uniform status for refugees or for persons eligible for subsidiary protection, and for the content of the protection granted*.

European Parliament & Council of the EU (2013).*Directive 2013/33/EU of the European Parliament and of the Council of 26 June 2013 laying down standards for the reception of applicants for international protection (recast)*. EUR-Lex. http://data.europa.eu/eli/dir/2013/33/oj/eng

Faist, T. (2006). The Migration-Security Nexus: International Migration and Security Before and After 9/11. In Y. M. Bodemann & G. Yurdakul (Eds.), *Migration, Citizenship, Ethnos* (pp. 103–119). Palgrave Macmillan US. https://doi.org/10.1057/9781403984678_6

Fassi, E., Lucarelli, S., & Ceccorulli, M. (Eds.). (2021). *The EU Migration System of Governance: Justice on the Move*. Springer International Publishing. https://doi.org/10.1007/978-3-030-53997-9_10

Frasca, E., & Gatta, F. L. (2022). Ebbs and Flows of EU Migration Law and Governance: A Critical Assessment of the Evolution of Migration Legislation and Policy in Europe. *European Journal of Migration and Law*, 24(1), 56–85. https://doi.org/10.1163/15718166-12340119

Freedman, J. (2016). Engendering Security at the Borders of Europe: Women Migrants and the Mediterranean 'Crisis.' *Journal of Refugee Studies*, 29(4), 568–582. https://doi.org/10.1093/jrs/few019

Freedman, J. (2019a). A Gendered Analysis of the European Refugee "Crisis." In C. Menjívar, M. Ruiz, & I. Ness (Eds.), *The Oxford Handbook of Migration Crises* (p. 0). Oxford University Press. https://doi.org/10.1093/oxfordhb/9780190856908.013.57

Freedman, J. (2019b). The uses and abuses of "vulnerability" in EU asylum and refugee protection: Protecting women or reducing autonomy? *Papeles Del CEIC, 2019*, 204. https://doi.org/10.1387/pceic.19525

Fukuyama, F. (1989). The End of History? *The National Interest, 16*, 3–18.

Goffman, E. (1974). *Frame analysis: An essay on the organization of experience* (pp. ix, 586). Harvard University Press.

Gomes, M. S., & Marques, R. R. (2021). Can securitization theory be saved from itself? A decolonial and feminist intervention. *Security Dialogue, 52*(1_suppl), 78–87. https://doi.org/10.1177/09670106211027795

Grappi, G. (2020). *Europe and the Contested Politics of Migration: Between Logistification and Global Justice* (SSRN Scholarly Paper No. 3557952). https://doi.org/10.2139/ssrn.3557952

Gray, H., & Franck, A. K. (2019a). Refugees as/at risk: The gendered and racialized underpinnings of securitization in British media

narratives. *Security Dialogue, 50*(3), 275–291. https://doi.org/10.1177/
0967010619830590

Gray, H., & Franck, A. K. (2019b). Refugees as/at risk: The gendered
and racialized underpinnings of securitization in British media
narratives. *Security Dialogue, 50*(3), 275–291. https://doi.org/10.1177/
0967010619830590

Guild, E., Carrera, S., Allsopp, J., Andrijasevic, R., Collyer, M., Dimitriadi,
A., Jokinen, A., Leerkes, A., Manieri, M. G., Muraszkiewicz, J., Ruete,
M., Spena, A., & Spencer, S. (2016). *Irregular Migration, Trafficking and
Smuggling of Human Beings: Policy Dilemmas in the EU. CEPS Paperback,
22 February 2016* (E. Guild & S. Carrera, Eds.). https://www.ceps.eu/
publications/irregular-migration-trafficking-and-smuggling-human-
beings-policy-dilemmas-eu

Hansen, L. (2000). The Little Mermaid's Silent Security Dilemma and the
Absence of Gender in the Copenhagen School. *Millennium: Journal of
International Studies, 29*(2), 285–306. https://doi.org/10.1177/0305829800
0290020501

Hintjens, H. (2019). Failed Securitisation Moves during the 2015 'Migration
Crisis.' *International Migration, 57*(4), 181–196. https://doi.org/10.1111/
imig.12588

Howell, A., & Richter-Montpetit, M. (2020). Is securitization theory racist?
Civilizationism, methodological whiteness, and antiblack thought
in the Copenhagen School. *Security Dialogue, 51*(1), 3–22. https://doi.
org/10.1177/0967010619862921

Hruschka, C., & Leboeuf, L. (2019). *Vulnerability Authors: A Buzzword
or a Standard for Migration Governance?* (No. 20; Population & Policy
Compact). https://population-europe.eu/files/documents/pb20_
vulnerability_web.pdf

Hudson, H. (2005). 'Doing' Security As Though Humans Matter: A
Feminist Perspective on Gender and the Politics of Human Security.
Security Dialogue, 36(2), 155–174. https://doi.org/10.1177/0967010605054642

Huysmans, J. (2000). The European Union and the Securitization of
Migration. *JCMS: Journal of Common Market Studies, 38*(5), 751–777.
https://doi.org/10.1111/1468-5965.00263

Justice, freedom and security. (n.d.). EUR-Lex. Retrieved May 24, 2023, from
https://eur-lex.europa.eu/summary/chapter/justice_freedom_security.
html?root_default=SUM_1_CODED%3D23

Karyotis, G. (2007). European Migration Policy in the Aftermath of September 11. *Innovation: The European Journal of Social Science Research*, *20*(1), 1–17. https://doi.org/10.1080/13511610701197783

Kebsi, J. (2021, October 22). *Colonial feminism and the un-liberation of women in Iraq*. Https://Www.Newarab.Com/; The New Arab. https://www.newarab.com/opinion/colonial-feminism-and-un-liberation-women-iraq

Khalil, Z.-. (2017, November 16). *Security for Whom? Unpacking the Gendered Impact of EU Securitized Migration*. Jadaliyya. https://www.jadaliyya.com/Details/34701

Lucarelli, S. (2021). The EU Migration System and Global Justice: An Introduction. In E. Fassi, S. Lucarelli, & M. Ceccorulli (Eds.), *The EU Migration System of Governance: Justice on the Move* (pp. 1–32). Springer International Publishing. https://doi.org/10.1007/978-3-030-53997-9_10

Luthman, I. (2017). *The Gendered Implications of Securitized Migration*: Uppsala Universitet.

Massari, A. (2021). Threatened, the Refugee as the Referent Object. In A. Massari (Ed.), *Visual Securitization: Humanitarian Representations and Migration Governance* (pp. 135–166). Springer International Publishing. https://doi.org/10.1007/978-3-030-71143-6_6

Mohanty, C. T. (1984). Under Western Eyes: Feminist Scholarship and Colonial Discourses. *Boundary 2*, *12/13*, 333–358. https://doi.org/10.2307/302821

Morán, J. J. D., & Teano, F. (2020). Gendering migration: Securitization and integration media narratives in Europe. *Revista de Investigación de La Cátedra Internacional Conjunta Inocencio III*, *1*(11), Article 11.

Moreno-Lax, V. (2018). The EU Humanitarian Border and the Securitization of Human Rights: The 'Rescue-Through-Interdiction/Rescue-Without-Protection' Paradigm. *JCMS: Journal of Common Market Studies*, *56*(1), 119–140. https://doi.org/10.1111/jcms.12651

Refugees and Migrants. Definitions. (2016, April 12). United Nations. https://refugeesmigrants.un.org/definitions

Sachseder, J., Stachowitsch, S., & Binder, C. (2022a). Gender, race, and crisis-driven institutional growth: Discourses of 'migration crisis' and the expansion of Frontex. *Journal of Ethnic and Migration Studies*, *48*(19), 4670–4693. https://doi.org/10.1080/1369183X.2022.2092461

Sachseder, J., Stachowitsch, S., & Binder, C. (2022b). Gender, race, and crisis-driven institutional growth: Discourses of 'migration crisis' and the expansion of Frontex. *Journal of Ethnic and Migration Studies, 48*(19), 4670–4693. https://doi.org/10.1080/1369183X.2022.2092461

Sanchez, G., Arrouche, K., Capasso, M., Dimitriadi, A., & Fakhry, A. (2021). Beyond Networks, Militias And Tribes: Rethinking Eu Counter-Smuggling Policy And Response. *Euromesco, 19.*

Schrover, M. (2019). Gender and Social Exclusion in European Migration Crisis: A Sociohistorical Perspective. In C. Menjívar, M. Ruiz, & I. Ness (Eds.), *The Oxford Handbook of Migration Crises* (p. 0). Oxford University Press. https://doi.org/10.1093/oxfordhb/9780190856908.013.12

Skjetne, V. S. B. (2019). *Combating trafficking in the face of the 'migrant crisis'* (No. 4; GLOBUS). ARENA Centre for European Studies.

Special meeting of the European Council, 23 April 2015. (2015, April 23). European Council. https://www.consilium.europa.eu/en/press/press-releases/2015/04/23/special-euco-statement/

Spivak, G. C. (1988). Can the Subaltern Speak? In *Marxism and the Interpretation of Culture* (pp. 271–314). Macmillan Education. https://abahlali.org/files/Can_the_subaltern_speak.pdf

Stachowitsch, S., & Sachseder, J. (2019). The gendered and racialized politics of risk analysis. The case of Frontex. *Critical Studies on Security, 7*(2), 107–123. https://doi.org/10.1080/21624887.2019.1644050

Stępka, M. (2022). EU Migration-Security Continuum. Investigating Security Frames Before the "Migration Crisis." In M. Stępka (Ed.), *Identifying Security Logics in the EU Policy Discourse: The "Migration Crisis" and the EU* (pp. 63–91). Springer International Publishing. https://doi.org/10.1007/978-3-030-93035-6_4

Tirman, J. (2006). Immigration and Insecurity: Post-9/11 Fear in the United States. *MIT Center for International Studies,* 1–4. https://doi.org/10.4337/9781781000700.00008

Turner, L. (2021). The Politics of Labeling Refugee Men as "Vulnerable." *Social Politics: International Studies in Gender, State & Society, 28*(1), 1–23. https://doi.org/10.1093/sp/jxz033

Turner, L. (2016, November 29). *Are Syrian Men Vulnerable Too? Gendering The Syria Refugee Response.* Middle East Institute. https://www.mei.edu/

publications/are-syrian-men-vulnerable-too-gendering-syria-refugee-response

UNHCR. (2023). *Global Report 2022. Ukraine.* Global Focus. https://reporting.unhcr.org/operational/situations/ukraine-situation

Universal Declaration of Human Rights. (1948). United Nations; United Nations. https://www.un.org/en/about-us/universal-declaration-of-human-rights

UNODC. (2019). *Women in Migrant-smuggling. A case-law analysis.* https://www.unodc.org/documents/human-trafficking/2021/Women_in_Migrant_Smuggling.pdf

Vatta, A. (2017). The EU Migration Policy between Europeanization and Re-Nationalization. In S. Baldin & M. Zago (Eds.), *Europe of Migrations: Policies, Legal Issues and Experiences* (pp. 13–31). EUT Edizioni Università di Trieste. https://www.openstarts.units.it/handle/10077/15218

Verloo, M., & Lombardo, E. (2007). Contested Gender Equality and Policy Variety in Europe: Introducing a Critical Frame Analysis Approach. In M. Verloo, *Multiple Meanings of Gender Equality: A Critical Frame Analysis of Gender Policies in Europe.* Central European University Press. http://ezproxy.unibo.it/login?url=https://search.ebscohost.com/login.aspx?direct=true&db=nlebk&AN=196610&site=ehost-live&scope=site

Welfens, N. (2020). Protecting Refugees Inside, Protecting Borders Abroad? Gender in the EU's Responses to the 'Refugee Crisis.' *Political Studies Review, 18*(3), 378–392. https://doi.org/10.1177/1478929919887349

Williams, P. D., & McDonald, M. (Eds.). (2023). *Security Studies: An Introduction* (4th ed.). Routledge. https://doi.org/10.4324/9781003247821

Appendix A

Codebook for Critical Frame Analysis of EU Migration Policies

Two different codebooks have been designed for the diagnosis and the prognosis of the problem. Each codebook has three levels, which in total count 4 arch-frames, 14 frames, and 9 subframes. Each arch-frame features several frames; frames may further contain subframes. Each code presents a general description and a specific example drawn from the dataset. The codebooks were utilized for the analysis conducted through the MAXQDA software.

DIAGNOSIS				
Arch-frame	Frame	Subframe	Description	Examples
Feminized vulnerability			Explicit reference to the vulnerability of women	"Criminal networks lure mainly women in vulnerable positions into an activity that appears to earn them 'easy money' but instead traps them in a web of exploitation and abuse."

(Continued)

(Continued)

	DIAGNOSIS			
Arch-frame	Frame	Subframe	Description	Examples
	Unaware & disinformed victims		Migrants are portrayed as unaware of the real dangers of smuggling and trafficking	"The Commission launched information and awareness raising campaigns to inform potential migrants about the risks of smuggling and irregular migration and to counter the narrative of smugglers."
	Deserving migrant		Migrants are portrayed as 'good' and worthy of support based on their perceived vulnerability	"There is emerging evidence that smugglers are facilitating the unauthorised movements of beneficiaries of international protection."
	'Womenand-children'		Migrant women are grouped into a monolithic body of vulnerability alongside children	"The EU should step up efforts to provide smuggled migrants, in particular vulnerable groups such as children and women."
	Sexual exploitation		Migrants are described as victims of sexual exploitation	"Trafficking for sexual exploitation, involving mainly women and girls as victims, is consistently reported as the prevalent form."
	Abuse & gender-based violence		Migrants are described as victims of abuse and/or other forms of violence	"The human rights of migrants are often gravely violated through abuse and exploitation."

DIAGNOSIS				
Arch-frame	Frame	Subframe	Description	Examples
Masculinized threat			Explicit reference to the dangerousness of men	
	Securitarian axis	Hypermasculinization of smugglers/traffickers	Smugglers/traffickers are referred to as characterized by stereotypically masculine traits	"Ruthless criminal networks organize the journeys of large numbers of migrants desperate to reach the EU."
		Criminal behavior	Smugglers/traffickers engage in criminal behavior	"Trafficking in human beings remains a highly profitable form of serious and organised crime."
			Migrants are portrayed as dangerous criminals, according to the migrant-criminal monograph	
		Violence	Smugglers/traffickers engage in violent behavior	"In some cases these networks have links with violent criminal organisations and/or armed groups."
			Migrants engage in violent behavior	
		Sexual predators	Smugglers/traffickers abuse migrant women	
			Migrants commit sexual assault and endanger European and fellow migrant women	

(Continued)

(Continued)

		DIAGNOSIS		
Arch-frame	Frame	Subframe	Description	Examples
	Socio-economic axis	*Homo oeconomicus*	Migrants are moved by economic motivations and become a threat to the EU's labor market and welfare system	"The possibility for irregular migrants to find a job in the informal economy is one of the key drivers of irregular migration."
		Financial gains	Smugglers/traffickers are moved by short-term and long-term profit	"To maximize their profits, smugglers often squeeze hundreds of migrants onto unseaworthy boats."
	Identitarian axis	'Pressure' frame	The increase in migratory flows, comprised of alien 'others', is a problem to be urgently addressed	"EU agencies work closely together with the authorities of Member States facing migratory pressures at the EU's external borders."
	Undeserving migrant		Migrants are portrayed as 'bad', denied the legal right to migration, and worthy of being 'sacrificed'	"The effective return and sustainable reintegration of those without a legal right to stay in the EU also contributes to reducing the incentives for irregular migration."
	Hidden exclusionary effect of vulnerability		Certain groups are explicitly defined vulnerable, meaning that others are implicitly excluded from such a definition	"Address the situation of vulnerable women, children and other groups, including the Roma."

DIAGNOSIS				
Arch-frame	Frame	Subframe	Description	Examples
Recognition of men as vulnerable			Explicit reference to the dangerousness of men	"Potential differences in the vulnerability of men and women to victimization and its impact on them are recognized."

PROGNOSIS				
Arch-frame	Frame	Subframe	Description	Examples
Securitization	Referent object	EU as a referent object	The securitarian approach to smuggling and trafficking identifies them as threats to the European Union	"Migrant-smuggling is a cross-border criminal activity that undermines the migration management objectives of the EU."
		Migrants as a referent object	The humanitarian approach to smuggling and trafficking identifies them as threats to migrants	"Migrant-smuggling is a cross-border criminal activity that puts the lives of migrants at risk, showing disrespect for human life and dignity."
	Securitized threat		The language framing the problem is clearly that of security	"Stepping up the fight against organized criminal networks by means including disrupting the business model and untangling the trafficking chain."

(Continued)

(Continued)

		PROGNOSIS		
Arch-frame	Frame	Subframe	Description	Examples
	Ordinary measures		Measures within the political sphere are employed to address the problem	"Stronger and closer cooperation with partner countries included support to law enforcement and judicial cooperation, capacity building in border management, information and awareness raising campaigns."
	Extraordinary measures		Measures within the military and defense spheres are employed to address the problem	"The EU and its Member States have mandated Common Security and Defense Policy (CSDP) missions over the past years to address security challenges related to irregular."

Appendix B

MAXQDA Critical Frame Analysis Results
Smuggling

The results showcase what proportion each frame comprises of the identified codes under a selected arch-frame, either of feminized vulnerability or of masculinized threat. In respect to the anti-smuggling governance, the policy documents analyzed were: EU Action Plan against Migrant Smuggling (2015–2020); 2017 REFIT evaluation of the EU legal framework against facilitation of unauthorized entry, transit and residence: the Facilitators Package; A renewed EU Action Plan against Migrant Smuggling (2021–2025).

Feminized vulnerability

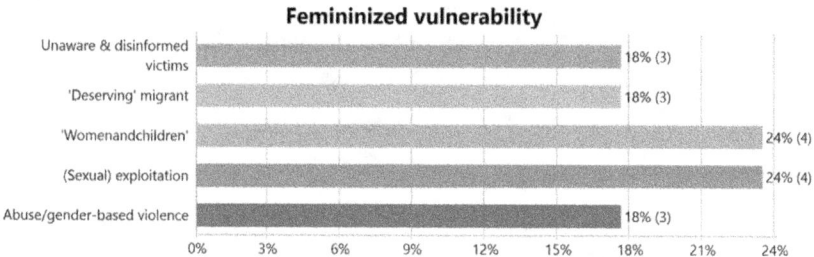

Femininized vulnerability

Frame	Value
Unaware & disinformed victims	18% (3)
'Deserving' migrant	18% (3)
'Womenandchildren'	24% (4)
(Sexual) exploitation	24% (4)
Abuse/gender-based violence	18% (3)

0% 3% 6% 9% 12% 15% 18% 21% 24%

Masculinized threat

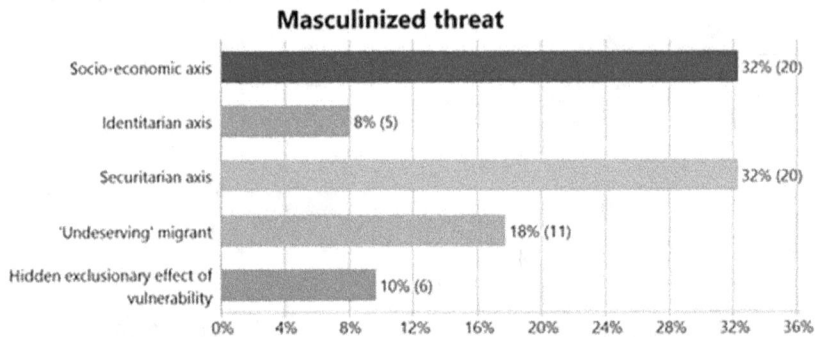

Masculinized threat

Socio-economic axis	32% (20)
Identitarian axis	8% (5)
Securitarian axis	32% (20)
'Undeserving' migrant	18% (11)
Hidden exclusionary effect of vulnerability	10% (6)

(Scale: 0%, 4%, 8%, 12%, 16%, 20%, 24%, 28%, 32%, 36%)

Trafficking

The results showcase what proportion each frame comprises of the identified codes under a selected arch-frame, either of feminized vulnerability or of masculinized threat. In respect to the anti-trafficking governance, the policy documents analyzed were: the EU Strategy towards the Eradication of Trafficking in Human Beings (2012–2016); 2017 Reporting on the follow-up to the EU Strategy towards the Eradication of trafficking in human beings and identifying further concrete actions; EU Strategy on Combatting Trafficking in Human Beings (2021- 2025); Fourth Report on the progress made in the fight against trafficking in human beings.

Feminized vulnerability

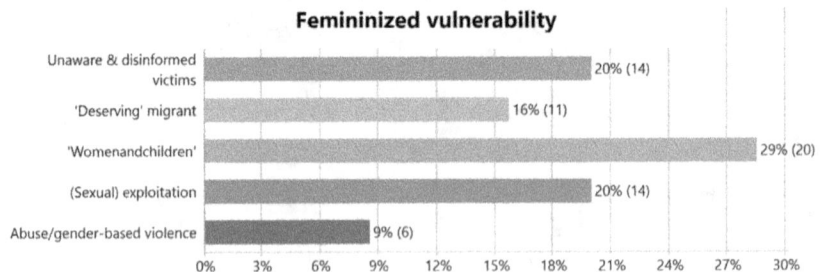

Femininized vulnerability

Unaware & disinformed victims	20% (14)
'Deserving' migrant	16% (11)
'Womenandchildren'	29% (20)
(Sexual) exploitation	20% (14)
Abuse/gender-based violence	9% (6)

(Scale: 0%, 3%, 6%, 9%, 12%, 15%, 18%, 21%, 24%, 27%, 30%)

Masculinized threat

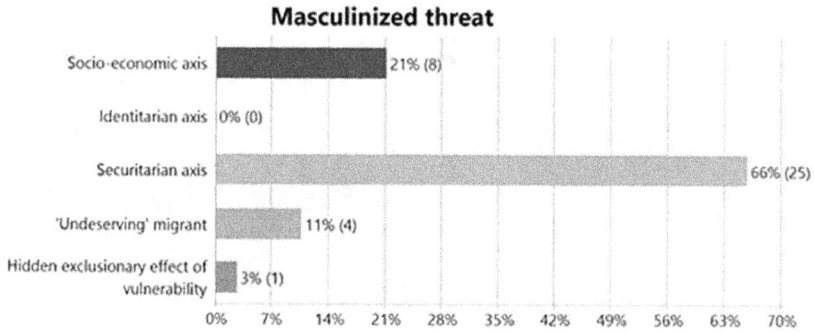

Masculinized threat

Socio-economic axis	21% (8)
Identitarian axis	0% (0)
Securitarian axis	66% (25)
'Undeserving' migrant	11% (4)
Hidden exclusionary effect of vulnerability	3% (1)

0% 7% 14% 21% 28% 35% 42% 49% 56% 63% 70%

Interkultureller Dialog

Edited by Annemarie Profanter

www.peterlang.com

www.ingramcontent.com/pod-product-compliance
Lightning Source LLC
Chambersburg PA
CBHW070351270326
41926CB00017B/4094